COOK
HOUSE

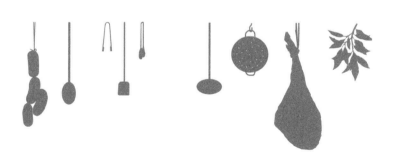

COOK HOUSE

ANNA HEDWORTH

HEAD
of ZEUS

An Anima Book

Contents

COOK HOUSE

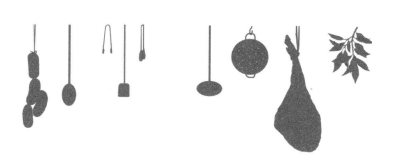

Introduction

After years of discontent, I finally plucked up the courage to leave my desk job and create a new career for myself – running a tiny restaurant in a shipping container, writing recipes, menu planning, greeting customers, growing my own produce, foraging and cooking every day. This book is not only filled with all the delicious recipes I have cooked along the way, but also tells the story of how it all panned out by way of anecdotes, tips and beach fires. I hope it will be an inspiration for the millions of others who dream of jumping ship and creating something of their own.

Five years ago I sat at a desk wondering how to get out, a story repeated the world over. I was working for a local architecture firm, an interesting and creative one at that, and although I still have a love for art and design, the actual nuts and bolts of the job just weren't for me… and when it comes to architecture the nuts and bolts are pretty important.

For a while I didn't know what the answer was, but it turns out that it was staring me in the face. Every minute away from my desk, and many covert minutes at my desk, I was planning meals, menus, events, get-togethers and feasts with family and friends.

I realized I wanted a job where I ate, cooked and fed people every day, but at that point in time I didn't know how to get there. However, step by step over the past few years I have made my way there; from feeling like I was in the wrong job entirely, to owning and running my own micro-restaurant.

Cook House began as a recipe blog and supper club, cooking for strangers in unusual locations, offering them an envelope at the end of each meal with a 'pay what you feel' vibe. It allowed me to test out my cooking skills, and try out this new life while still getting a pay cheque from architecture. It was a tough few years as I was basically working two jobs, but I loved every second of it.

It became a permanent space in 2014 and has been open for four years. Today, as I write, I am about to open in new premises, but it all started with my love of food, some local markets and a couple of second-hand shipping containers. It is a path I have forged for myself, using my own efforts and ideas, and it's worked. It grew from a desire to bring people delicious food and encourage them to cook it too. I wanted to share this story in the hope that others, who are still sat at their desks, searching for a way out, will see that it is entirely possible to forge a new life for themselves.

About Cook House

Cook House is more than just the name of a restaurant or a book. It embodies the idea of being in my kitchen, cooking for people, feeding people and the conviviality of the table.

Today I have a beautiful restaurant where I cook every day, housed in two black shipping containers. It has won awards and gained national recognition. It has my collection of food postcards on the walls, shades of pale blue on the furniture and walls, herbs growing in the sunny garden, strings of little lights, a lovely atmosphere, shelves lined with pickles, ferments and home-made vinegars, and a little pot-bellied wood burner for winter. It's exactly what I wanted it to be.

The neon 'Service' sign flickers on each morning and customers start to arrive. The menu is on the wall on a little chalkboard – usually about six savoury dishes and a couple of puddings – that changes all the time. Working this way has allowed me to cook, test and refine hundreds of recipes over the past few years.

The containers have an open-plan layout centred around a small kitchen. Diners can chat to me as I cook, ask how to make things and where to source ingredients. They can sit in the garden where I grow herbs and vegetables, or come along to meet guest chefs and eat their food. They can meet new people at a long-table supper club or event, even if they feel a bit apprehensive on arrival. They can come to a demonstration by my butcher or just stop for a coffee. I'm trying to develop a way of engaging with place and food that goes further than just relaxed dining.

We cook at Cook House six days a week, but also travel around the region hosting dinners and events in beautiful spots in Northumberland – from castles to islands, beaches to breweries. A sense of place and a nod to the location is hugely important to my menus: enhancing the beauty and joy of these experiences with the food.

My food is led by the seasons, what the local producers and farms have to offer and what nature is currently offering in the fields and woods. I focus on taste, texture and colour and a process of serving food that is ethical and good for you but not faddy or limited by theme or cuisine. As well as my desire to never put anything in the bin (it can always be turned into something), my cooking is also informed by the limitations of my tiny 'domestic' kitchen. I have achieved what I have so far with the most limited budget of equipment and smallest of spaces, which just goes to show that anyone could do this...

About Me

I have a huge passion for cooking, it is the first and foremost reason why all of this has happened. I genuinely believe that food, eating and conviviality should be of huge importance in people's lives. It can bring such joy. I cook for people to enjoy themselves.

As owner and chef I am in the kitchen a lot, but I am also managing bookings, orders, social media, press, accounts and everything else that goes with running a small food business. Unlike most restaurant owners, I am self-taught. I have learnt everything I know by just trying things out – whether that is at markets, dinners at home or feeding five hundred people. The recipes in this book are the ones I have developed over the years – a genuine record of the whole process.

I like food that is delicious and interesting, which has a good balance of sweet, savoury and sharp flavours, of texture and crunch, and which is seasonal, fresh and tasty. I favour cooking with as few pans as possible, as little mess as possible and as little faff as possible. Most of my recipes are in line with this, with occasional larger fun projects.

Cook House is within walking distance of my house. I live with my other half Adrian and stepdaughter Flo. I walk to work most days, picking up ingredients from the market or the shops along the way, and planning out the day ahead.

I post on my recipe blog The Grazer as much as possible, as well as writing for other food publications. I founded a local farmers' market, Jesmond Food Market, which draws thousands of visitors each month. I wanted to do something to show the people of the North how proud of and well fed they can be by their own region.

I run supper clubs and occasional chef takeovers or collaborations at Cook House, teaming up with other local talented chefs to cook together, and also invite other chefs from around the country to venture up here.

I find myself outdoors as often as time allows, either picking wild food, tidying my out-of-control allotment or building fires to cook on in beautiful spots. My love of preserving, fermenting and any other DIY food projects I've dreamt up take up my remaining free minutes.

I love what I do, it is incredibly hard work compared to my old job, and takes up all my time, but there is no longer a difference between life and work: it is all one thing. It's all about food, cooking, growing, learning, and I love it. Luckily, everyone else in my household does too!

In the Beginning

I should have known when I was excitedly looking up how to make butter from scratch one day at work instead of drawing construction details for a cinema that I was in the wrong profession. I suppose I did know that, I just didn't know what to do about it. Ideas pinged into my head like small fireworks while sat at the computer; 'BUTTER!' my brain would shout, and then I'd be lost online, looking at different opinions on butter making; 'RICOTTA!', thumbing through books at home trying to find the best thinking on fresh cheese. 'VERMOUTH!', wouldn't it be lovely to have my own house vermouth... I should have realized sooner.

My family have always been into eating and gathering round a big dining table, but I only started to dabble in the kitchen when I went to university. My efforts prior to that were poor to say the least, my signature dish being one of tinned tuna, rice, cheese and toast.

My childhood memories of food are classics: my mum made a great shepherd's pie and peas or toad in the hole. My favourite meal was chunky chicken and rice – tinned chicken in a white sauce from Marks & Spencer, heated through with plain rice; or 'picky bits', which meant slices of strawberries, cheese, garlic sausage and cucumber made into a face on a plate – I couldn't get enough of those faces.

I stayed at my granny and grandad's house quite often and my granny was always cooking. She had one of those little hatches that opened up between the kitchen and the dining table and we would play shops while she cooked. I'd go to the hatch and ask her what was on sale today and she would list the entire contents of the cupboards and fridge and then I'd say, 'Nothing today thank you!' and walk away laughing every time. I found it hilarious.

There were no rules at their house and I was allowed anything I wanted. At breakfast, while my grandad ate his half grapefruit with a sprinkle of sugar followed by a full English, I would construct my Weetabix bowl. This was comprised of a layer of sugar, two Weetabix, another layer of sugar, milk and then extra sugar to fill in any gaps that didn't look sugary enough. No one commented.

My granny made a brilliant sticky blackberry and apple crumble. We would gather blackberries for hours while walking the dog and fill the freezer with them. Banana syllabub was the fancy dessert that came out for guests; you just helped yourself to a choc-ice on more casual occasions. Other favourites at their house were really tasty lentil soup, a funny spaghetti

bake thing that I loved and white baguettes with as much butter as I fancied. I always helped in the kitchen and my favourite job was to make the Yorkshire pudding batter, which had to be beaten in a certain way with a wooden spoon until it made just the right sound: a repeating plop, plop, plop like someone was doing little belly flops in it.

There was always a Club biscuit on the go, or a Penguin, a big bar of Fruit & Nut or a small bowl of peanuts and raisins on a table, not put out for people, just there all the time. We would have big family gatherings for Sunday lunch where there were sometimes so many people that anything in the house that could be used as a chair was employed. Often a tall uncle would end up on the 'pouffe', his chin level with the table. Plates of food just kept appearing through the hatch, and even the dog got his own full Sunday dinner in a bowl. I think this is where my love for gathering and eating began – I remember my grandparents' house and everything I ate there very fondly.

I didn't know what I wanted to do when I was nearing the end of school. I went to see the careers advice teacher and she did a little questionnaire with me and at the end told me I should be a geography teacher. She was a geography teacher. Maybe she just said this to everyone? Who knows, but one thing I knew clearly was that I shouldn't be a geography teacher.

I wanted to study fine art, and after school enrolled on an art foundation course. I was good at graphics, lifedrawing, portraits and photography. I wanted to go to art school, but my parents' fears and, to some extent, my own led me to looking at courses with 'a job at the end of them'. Sitting round on a Friday night with a take out from the 'Golden Curry' in our bombshell of a post-school flat share, surrounded by piles of university prospectuses, my flatmate Sarah said, 'Why don't you do architecture? That's a job,' and it was decided...

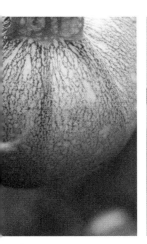

I now know it was never the right thing to have done, but I didn't know what else to do and felt quite panicked by it all. It seemed a sensible decision at the time… I got through the course; I didn't love it, except that initial stage of design, which was research, sketching, drawing and looking at beautiful works by other people. Details of how to actually build the thing left me cold. My course was at Edinburgh College of Art and I watched the art students with envy, but soldiered on regardless.

This was when I began to cook, however, albeit with low levels of success. We lived next to a really good deli, fishmonger and butcher, which I was always wandering into with interest. I remember a 'dinner party', which was a thinly veiled excuse to invite over a boy that my flatmate had an eye on, with some additional guests and food as cover. I don't remember if love came to the fore that evening but I do recall the laksa-style prawn dish that we accidentally made so incredibly hot, it was basically inedible. We gradually added more and more milk to cool it down until it was just a fiery milk soup with some overcooked prawns in the bottom.

As part of our course we were meant to work for a year in an architectural practice, so when the time came I found a job in Newcastle. I found myself in a large office, seventy or eighty people, all in one room – all men, except for the secretaries. No one spoke to me, I might as well have been a pot plant. It was utterly depressing. I don't know how long I lasted, maybe a month, but it was torture. I left and booked a flight to Greece. I spent the rest of the year working in a chaotic Mexican restaurant in Corfu for a pound an hour, blissfully happy.

SOUPS

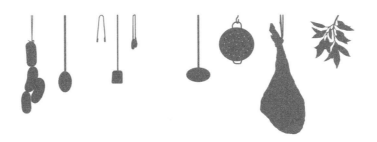

Soups

At Cook House, our soups are full of flavour and often topped with tasty oils or fresh herbs, seeds or nuts to create texture. I often serve them as a small course at our supper clubs in little cups, often with a Butter and Cardamom Bun (page 272) on the side, or a truffle cheese toasty. Soup doesn't have to be dull – it can bring joy!

Your base stocks will give real depth of flavour to the soup and they really do make a difference. If you are poaching a chicken for a pie or a salad or simmering a ham, then keep the leftover stock in labelled old cleaned-out milk bottles or yoghurt pots in the freezer. This takes all of the work out of a soup.

To make stock specifically for soup you need to be gentle. Chop onions, carrots, celery, leeks and add to a pan of cold water, then add black peppercorns and a couple of bay leaves. For vegetable stock just stop here and simmer this very gently for about 40 minutes. For chicken stock, add a whole chicken or chicken wings along with the vegetables and simmer so it is only just moving, for an hour or so. If using a whole chicken, you can use the resulting poached chicken for another dish. If you are cooking ham hocks, then the leftover stock is also great to use for soup or if you prefer to make a ham stock just for soup, then simmer some ham bones very gently for an hour.

Season your soups carefully – it can make all the difference. A large pot of soup will often need a little more salt than you think. If it is too rich, add a squeeze of lemon juice or if it seems bland, add a pinch more spice, pepper or salt. A spoonful of sugar can lift a pepper or tomato soup. Take a bit of time over these tweaks at the end and you will be rewarded.

I hadn't come across much lovage until a friend gave me a cutting of their plant to put in my allotment, and I'm now a massive fan. You won't find it in the shops, so you will need to make friends with allotment owners or grow it yourself. It has a rich peppery flavour and belongs to the celery and parsley family, but has much more character.

This soup is silky and comforting. Top with fresh wild garlic oil and some nutty toasted seeds and serve with buttery toast.

Lovage and Leek Soup with Wild Garlic Oil

Place the onions in a large pan with the olive oil, butter and add a large pinch of salt, then add the leeks, lovage stems and shallots and cook over a medium heat for 10 minutes.

Add the potatoes and stir well. Pour in enough of the stock to just cover all of the vegetables and simmer for 30 minutes, or until the potatoes and vegetables are soft.

Add the lovage leaves to the pan and simmer for a few more minutes, then using a stick blender, blend until everything is smooth and silky, adding more stock or water until it is the desired consistency. I like my soups very smooth, about as thick as double cream. Season it as you blend it, adding a generous turning of pepper as well as a good few pinches of salt. Continue to simmer the soup after blending for a couple of minutes.

While the soup is simmering, make the wild garlic oil. Add the wild garlic leaves to a small blender with a pinch of salt and the olive oil and blend until very smooth.

Top the soup with a generous drizzle of the wild garlic oil and a handful of toasted pumpkin seeds.

SERVES 4

- 2 onions, roughly chopped
- 1 tbsp olive oil
- 20g butter
- 2 leeks, trimmed and sliced
- 3 large stems of lovage, leaves picked and stems roughly chopped
- 2 shallots, peeled and roughly chopped
- 2 large floury potatoes, peeled and cut into cubes
- 1 litre chicken or ham stock
- salt and pepper
- toasted pumpkin seeds, for topping

WILD GARLIC OIL

- 50g wild garlic leaves
- pinch of sea salt
- 50ml olive oil

EQUIPMENT

- stick blender
- blender

Alternatives

nettles; sorrel; spinach

NOTES

If you can't find any lovage, this soup is still delicious with young nettles. Pick them when they first come up in spring, but make sure you wear gloves as they will sting. Likewise if you can't find any wild garlic, use rocket or dill instead.

The wild garlic oil makes more than you need for this recipe, but it keeps for months in a clean jar in the fridge.

This soup works best with a really good shellfish stock, so plan ahead and next time you are having some prawns, langoustines, crab or lobster, keep all the scraps and make your own. I feel like I'm winning at life when I have different stocks ready in the freezer... You start this recipe by 'jugging' the kippers, which is essentially just covering them with the hot stock. I think people used to use a jug and dip the kippers into it held by the tail to cook them briefly – hence the name.

Kipper and Potato Soup

SERVES 2

- 1 litre shellfish stock or fish stock cubes
- 1 kipper, such as Craster or similar
- 1 tbsp butter
- 2 banana shallots, peeled and finely sliced
- white of 1 leek, trimmed and finely sliced
- 1 large baking potato, peeled and diced
- 1/4 tsp curry powder
- salt and pepper
- 50ml white wine
- 50ml double cream
- few chives, for topping

EQUIPMENT
- rimmed baking tray or jug
- blender

Alternatives
smoked haddock

Bring the stock to a simmer in a pan until hot. Place the kipper in a rimmed baking tray or in a jug that's roughly the same size and pour over the hot stock, then cover with clingfilm and set aside.

Melt the butter in a pan large enough to ultimately hold all the soup, then add the shallots and leek. Add the potato and stir to coat the vegetables in the butter. Add the curry powder and a pinch of salt and pepper, then leave to soften for about 10 minutes, stirring occasionally.

Pour the white wine into the pan and turn the heat up briefly to cook off the alcohol. Waft the escaping steam towards your nose to check to see when the alcohol has gone. Add the stock that the kipper has been sat in, which is now a delicious double fish stock and gently cook until the veg are tender.

Meanwhile, flake the meat from the kipper, taking care to get rid of as many bones as possible and set the meat aside.

Add the cream to the potato mixture in the pan and blend until smooth. Check the soup to see if it needs salt. I also like to add lots of pepper. Finally, add the flaked kipper meat to the soup and heat through gently. Serve with a few chopped chives on top. This soup keeps very well for a few days in the fridge.

I owe Diana Henry a drink, because this is a tweaked version of her recipe that I decided to make on television as part of Cook House appearing on what turned out to be a beautiful programme called Hidden Restaurants. I cooked this in the kitchen with Michel Roux Junior, while shaking in my boots, but it turned out to be the best boost to business we ever had. I will therefore always remember this soup. We topped it with a chunky nasturtium pesto that Michel made– I should probably buy him a drink too while I'm at the bar...

Chilled Summer Garden Soup with Nasturtium Pesto

Put all the ingredients into a blender and blend until smooth. You may have to do this in batches depending on the size of your blender. Check the seasoning, it does not need much salt or pepper, just a little, but it may benefit from a tiny bit more vinegar. Chill the soup thoroughly before serving.

Serve the soup with a drizzle of fresh peppery Nasturtium and Pumpkin Seed Pesto or Rocket Pesto (see page 46).

SERVES 4

- 1 cucumber, peeled and chopped
- 2 very fresh young courgettes, chopped
- 50g walnuts
- 50g blanched almonds
- 4 garlic cloves
- 3 spring onions
- 3 tbsp chopped chives
- 3 tbsp chopped mint
- 3 tbsp chopped dill
- 2 tbsp chopped tarragon
- pinch of chilli flakes
- 50g stale sourdough bread, crusts removed
- 250ml weak chicken stock
- 200g live full-fat natural yoghurt
- 100ml extra virgin olive oil
- juice of 1/2 lemon
- 2 tbsp white balsamic vinegar
- salt and pepper

EQUIPMENT
- blender

We once spent a weekend barbecuing for over five hundred people and I wildly misjudged how many red peppers we needed to make the Romesco sauce (see page 167). They were also incredibly expensive, so as soon as we were done feeding the five hundred we needed to come up with something to do with the multiple boxes of peppers I had over-ordered, and this soup emerged. Based loosely on the flavours of Romesco, which I adore, it is rich and warming, deep red, smoky with paprika and rosemary, but also fresh and summery from the red peppers.

Red Pepper, Paprika and Rosemary Soup with Sourdough Croûtons

SERVES 4-6

- 10 red peppers, chopped with seeds and stalks removed
- 50ml olive oil, plus extra for tossing
- salt and pepper
- 2 onions, peeled and roughly chopped
- 3 garlic cloves, peeled and crushed
- 1 sprig of rosemary, leaves picked
- 1 tbsp sweet smoked paprika
- 1 litre chicken stock

CROUTONS

- 2 slices of stale sourdough bread, crusts removed and bread torn into cubes
- olive oil
- salt and pepper

EQUIPMENT

- large roasting tray
- baking tray
- stick blender

Preheat the oven to 200°C/400°F/Gas 6. Place the peppers in a large roasting tray, toss in olive oil, season with salt and roast in the oven for 25 minutes.

Meanwhile, mix the bread cubes with olive oil and salt and pepper, then spread them out on a baking tray and bake for 10 minutes, or until they are golden and crispy. Set aside.

Sweat the onions in the olive oil in a large pan over a medium heat. Add the crushed garlic, a large pinch of salt and the rosemary leaves and cook for 10–15 minutes until soft and golden. Add the paprika, then add the peppers when they are done. Pour in enough chicken stock to just cover everything and simmer for 15 minutes.

Blitz the soup with a stick blender until it is very smooth – you may have to add more stock. Season to taste with salt and pepper and add more paprika, if you like.

Top with the sourdough croûtons or a few toasted hazelnuts and some toasted seeds. A drizzle of roasted garlic oil also works well.

I love a trip to the Chinese supermarket – especially the fruit and vegetable section. This is where I first found fresh turmeric. It looks like a small ginger root with browny-orange skin and a bright vibrant orange inside that smells earthy, but with hints of ginger as it belongs to the same plant family.

This is an earthy, vibrant soup with spicy depth and warmth. It is lovely served with a drizzle of curry oil and a scattering of nigella seeds.

Fresh Turmeric, Saffron and Potato Soup with Curry Oil

Place the leeks and the onions in a large pan with a generous splash of olive oil and a large pinch of salt and sweat for around 15 minutes on a low heat, stirring occasionally, until soft and turning golden.

Add the saffron, turmeric and chilli flakes and cook for a few more minutes. Add the diced potatoes and butter and cook for another 10 minutes.

Pour in enough water to just cover everything and simmer until the potatoes are completely soft. Season generously with salt and pepper, then blend until very smooth. You may need to add more water.

To make the curry oil, toast the curry powder in a dry frying pan for 1–2 minutes until you can smell it. Add the oil, garlic, ginger, bay leaf and salt to the pan, then remove from the heat and leave to infuse and cool. When it is cool, strain it through a sieve. It will keep in a jar for months.

To serve, top the soup with a generous splash of curry oil and a scattering of nigella seeds.

SERVES 4-6

SOUP
- 4 leeks, trimmed and sliced
- 4 onions, peeled and chopped
- olive oil, for cooking
- salt and pepper
- 1 large pinch of saffron threads
- 4-cm piece of fresh turmeric, peeled and grated or 1 tsp ground turmeric
- pinch of chilli flakes
- 6 medium potatoes, peeled and diced
- 20g butter
- 1 litre water approximately
- nigella seeds

CURRY OIL
- 1 tbsp medium curry powder
- 100ml olive oil
- 1 garlic clove, peeled and crushed
- 1 slice of fresh ginger
- 1 bay leaf
- pinch of salt

EQUIPMENT
- blender

How To...

Pack a Boat for Dinner on an Island

The Farne Islands sit about a mile off the coast of Northumberland, and in 2013 the National Trust approached me to put together a dinner at sea. We hosted five dinners and sailing home at sunset with happy guests and dolphins is one of my favourite moments yet.

01 **Buy large waterproof boxes and strong tape.** Wrap everything in bubble wrap and newspaper – just in case the waves get up. Tape down all the lids, there will be no retrieving the cake stand if it goes overboard.

02 **Remember everything** – there are no shops and no back-up plans. Make list after list and check and then double check. There will still be a moment when someone shouts 'MUSTARD' with panic in their voice.

03 **Take as much as you need, but also as little as possible.** Assess the weight of everything. You will have to lift it all into and out of the boat and carry it across the island.

04 **Unpack and organize yourself** as quickly as possible. Put everything in its place and stick to a plan for where the stuff goes. It will save you time and stress to know instantly where things are. God help anyone who moves the spatula.

05 **Work out what to do** when you arrive and no water comes out of the taps. There will be unique and unusual problems to navigate. Don't panic, improvise.

06 **Figure out how to serve the food** as efficiently as possible. This may be in the knowledge that the kitchen is separated from the table in the chapel by a nesting site of arctic terns that like to dive-bomb your head and have very sharp beaks.

07 **Serve huge piles of seafood** plucked straight from the sea and lots of wine and hope no one notices that you forgot to bring the menus.

08 **It is always about giving people the best experience,** and enjoying it yourself. No-one will care that there was no mustard, they will care that they ate delicious lobster, dined in an ancient chapel, met interesting people and sailed home with dolphins at sunset.

I Hate My Job

I stuck it out and finished my degree and found myself working for a small creative architecture firm in Newcastle. The projects were interesting, the people were nice and to begin with I enjoyed it. Over eight years I learnt a lot about design, interiors and graphics that I carry with me even now and this put me at an advantage when designing my own interiors, table settings, logos, websites and much more.

In the office, I obsessively read food blogs at lunchtime – there was quite a trend for them at the time, new ones constantly popping up that I bookmarked and pored over. I read design, photography and lifestyle blogs too. It was all quite new to me and it felt like buying all of your favourite magazines at once.

After having a go at designing a blog for the office, which I was pretty pleased with, I set about working on my own, drawing inspiration from all the ones I followed. I particularly loved following blogs that eventually became books...

I learnt all I needed to know about setting up a blog online and even dabbled in a bit of code to customize my own. The name was the hardest thing and it was my other half, Adrian, who came up with it, based around the idea of what a food-based newspaper would be called: *The Grazer*, as in *The Times*, *The Oracle*, etc. It has now become something people call me; I am 'The Grazer', which I really hate, but what can you do!

I was very happy with the website. It looked clean, clear and fresh – an organized home for my recipes. The title block was one of my photos of langoustines that I loved and would become one of my signature snaps. I was excited when I realized I would no longer lose all the precious scraps of paper and notes I was collecting, as I now had a beautiful online archive for all my food ideas.

I snapped pictures of salt and pepper squid, ate it, wrote a bit about it, uploaded it and then waited... and people looked. I remember laughing when a hundred people had been on the site. To be fair, it may just have been me and my dad refreshing all the time – he checks it constantly and chastises me when I haven't updated it often enough. These days, lots of people use it and it's a great feeling. People send me pictures of what they have made from it, and when people ask for recipes at Cook House I can direct them there.

Holding dinners at home had graduated to the point where I would invite up to fourteen people, which was literally the maximum the room would hold, with little or no space for moving around. Friends sat on chairs of various heights and strengths. I printed menus, made placecards and worked on four-, five- or six-course menus. I remember one based around Claudia Roden's book *Arabesque*. The menu was printed on a background of faded Moroccan tiles and we ate pastries, stuffed dates, tagines, pilafs and pistachio and orange blossom puddings; I think it might have been my birthday – any excuse, it was delicious regardless.

Claudia Roden, Sam and Sam Clarke, Elizabeth David, the guys from Joe Beef, Margot and Fergus Henderson were all my heroes and I pored over their books trying to absorb all their knowledge, tips and recipes. I read extensively and enthusiastically, not only recipes but also food writing, theory, history and anthropology. All of my spare time was full of food, cooking and learning as much as I could.

Work trundled on and in the back of my mind I was starting to form ideas about how I could escape. I didn't enjoy any of it and was forever looking for a distraction. I felt miserable and I didn't do well. There were times when I just ignored it and put my head down and got on with the work, and times when I ended up in tears. I looked into applying for other jobs, variations on a theme of design, interiors, graphics, trends, but I couldn't find the answer. I couldn't find the job that I would love *and* be good at...

In the kitchen, however, I had hours of patience. Learning, finding out how to do stuff, food science, chopping, faffing about, testing things out – nothing seemed like a big deal, it was all just very enjoyable. Trying to fathom my way through becoming an architect, however, was like wearing my pyjamas in a swimming pool.

I found true joy in food; cooking at home, cooking for more and more people, starting my own recipe blog – they were all distractions to begin with, but became my total passion, which would ultimately take me down a new road.

One of my architecture projects around this time was to set up a small gallery and events space using a couple of donated shipping containers saved from scrap on a derelict site in the Ouseburn –a creative 'up and coming' area just outside Newcastle's city centre. I worked on it with enthusiasm and found it interesting and creative. It became a lovely space quite quickly, even before it was fully fitted out, with stunning light, surrounded by trees on a quiet sunny street.

I started to put together a calendar of events that would take place there. I curated a design shop, a pop-up sewing bee, a space invaders games night, a street market and ultimately a programme of supper clubs...

While working on the containers in my day job, I had entered into the world of markets and street food in my side life. This was my next project after getting my food blog up and running. I was frustrated by the lack of food culture going on in Newcastle. I looked at London and it was streets ahead.

After a particularly depressing visit to a local food fair, which was very busy, but like a corporate conveyor belt of food, in an awful soulless venue that I couldn't wait to get out of, I decided to do something about it myself.

I wanted joy, and real people to hear stories about where things were made, about sheep, cows and bees. So I set out to do it myself, starting with a small market called Spring Graze in a local tennis hall. I'm thankful that traders had the faith in me to attend; some of them are still at my markets today. That first market was exactly what I had hoped for. It was about people and stories and a love of food, it was charming, a really enjoyable day. I went on to organize more and more: Summer Graze, Autumn Graze and the Ouseburn Festival Feast, which was a street-long food festival based in the event space at the containers.

The markets were a right faff to organize. I was setting up each table, bench, chair and sign myself and dropping flyers I had designed through thousands of doors, but I felt like I was doing something worthwhile: they were busy, successful and enjoyable events that people flocked to.

Today there is something like that going on every weekend in Newcastle and I feel like we have moved with, if not ahead of, the crowd as a city. I run my monthly Jesmond Food Market, which spans an old Victorian bridge in a local park, constantly trying to keep it full with the very best producers, chefs and street food vendors in the region. It's a long way from that tennis hall, but in many ways keeps the ethos and feel of what I first set out to do.

SAUCES
& DIPS

Sauces & Dips

A punchy garlicky aïoli with roast chicken, a fresh pesto drizzled over a beetroot salad or a smoky yoghurt to dip your lamb chops in; these accompaniments can lift simple meals into a different league. They all keep very well in the fridge, so when I'm organized I will have fresh pesto, aïoli, cumin yoghurt and a salad dressing in the fridge, or even if I'm disorganized they are all quick to make.

At Cook House all our salads come dressed in a delicious house dressing, which people constantly ask how to make. It is simple and adds so much flavour to what could be incredibly boring. We have converted multiple people who 'don't like salad', which is a good feeling.

If you are lighting the barbecue I would definitely recommended a good aïoli and a smoky aubergine yoghurt to go with your meats, salads and breads. Toss your vegetables in the anchovy dressing or in a powerful pesto and you'll add flavour and depth to simple meals.

The following sauces and dips are all made with fresh ingredients, so for more condiments and ketchups see the larder section (pages 278–308).

I remember making my first mayonnaise following Elizabeth David's instructions and being super proud of the science happening before my eyes. Give it a go, as it is so easy and satisfying. It can be flavoured any way you wish but I have given you a few suggestions.

Mayonnaise

MAKES 200ml

- 1 fresh egg
- 1 egg yolk
- 1 tsp Dijon mustard
- 1 tsp white wine vinegar
- pinch of salt
- about 100ml olive oil

EQUIPMENT
- small blender

This will take you about 5 minutes, and it is really much easier than you think. If you can't be bothered to whisk, it works very well in a small blender.

Mayonnaise likes all the equipment to be very clean, a bit like meringues. Add all the ingredients, except the olive oil, to a large clean bowl or to a small blender and whisk everything together thoroughly.

Slowly pour the olive oil in a very thin steady stream into the mix, whisking vigorously. Or add it, a little at a time, to the blender. The aim is to disperse all the oil molecules into the mix so it emulsifies and becomes thick, so you need to go for it with the whisk. The mixture will start to thicken the more oil you add, so keep going until you have a nice thick mayonnaise. Taste for seasoning, adding a little more salt, vinegar or mustard if you think it needs it.

If for some reason the mayonnaise 'splits' and it looks like it has separated, you can rescue it by adding an egg yolk to a new clean bowl and then slowly whisking in the split mixture, as you did the oil.

- Lemon: Add extra lemon juice at the end and whisk in. This goes very well with poached prawns, langoustines or lobster.

- English Mustard: Add twice the amount of English mustard at the beginning instead of Dijon. It goes very well in a ham sandwich or with salt beef.

- Wild Garlic: Blend or chop in a handful of wild garlic at the end. This is delicious in devilled eggs or an egg mayo sandwich.

- Dill: Blend or chop in a handful of dill at the end. It's great with roasted new potatoes and fennel or poached salmon.

On the face of it aïoli is just mayonnaise with garlic added to it, but in reality it is so much more than that. Aïoli is life to me. I struggle to look people in the eye who ask for our Cook House chicken salad without it. I always have some in the fridge at home. Dip anything into it and you're immediately having a better time: fritters, croquettes, wings, sandwiches, roast veg, salad – and then flavouring it makes it even better!

Aïoli

To make the aïoli, follow all the instructions for the mayonnaise on page 42, but add a clove of garlic at the beginning. Grate it into the mix if you are doing it by hand or just pop it into the blender if using one.

- Coriander: Separately blend a large handful of coriander with the garlic, a pinch of salt and some olive oil until you have a very fine paste, then whisk this into your aïoli. This is excellent with roast pork belly.

- Sriracha: Whisk in 1 teaspoon sriracha (spicy Thai chilli sauce) at the end. Taste and add more to suit. This is great with roast chicken, on a burger or for dipping chips into.

- Gochujang: Whisk in 1 teaspoon gochujang (a fermented red chilli paste from Korea, which is more flavourful than hot) at the end. It is great with the Korean-style Chicken Skewers on page 161, the BBQ Bavette on page 156 or for dipping fresh radishes into.

- Curried: Whisk in 1 teaspoon toasted curry powder at the end. This is amazing with roasted Brussels sprouts (see page 77) or grilled fish.

MAKES 200ml

- 1 fresh egg
- 1 egg yolk
- 1 tsp Dijon mustard
- 1 tsp white wine vinegar
- 1 garlic clove, peeled and grated
- pinch of salt
- 100ml olive oil

EQUIPMENT
- small blender

I use these quick pestos in a variety of ways, quickly whizzing up any greens or herbs I have in the fridge to coat pasta, drizzle over hot beetroot, new potatoes or greens, spoon on to salads with nuts and goat's cheese, spread over some puff pastry to form the base of a tasty tart or on top of soups. They are versatile and very tasty, deep with herbs, toasted nuts or seeds and a punch of garlic.

I'm calling these pestos, but I rarely use cheese, and I also make them in a small blender so Italian purists should probably look away now.

Pestos

MAKES 200ml

- 1 garlic clove
- pinch of salt and pepper
- splash of olive oil to start, then more to desired consistency

MINT AND ALMOND
- 2 large handfuls of mint
- 30g blanched almonds
- 1 tsp red wine vinegar

DILL AND HAZELNUT
- 2 large handfuls of dill
- 30g toasted hazelnuts

ROCKET AND WALNUT
- 2 handfuls of rocket
- 30g toasted walnuts

NASTURTIUM AND PUMPKIN SEED
- 25g nasturtium leaves
- 6 mint leaves
- 10 nasturtium seed pods
- 25g toasted pumpkin seeds

EQUIPMENT
- small blender

Place all the ingredients in a small blender and blitz. Check the consistency and add more olive oil depending if you want a thick or a thin pesto. Leave chunky to top stews and soups or blend until very fine for pasta and salads.

- Mint and Almond: Delicious with lamb chops, pea and asparagus salads or Burrata.

- Dill and Hazelnut: Serve with grilled fish, poached salmon or on top of creamy soups.

- Rocket and Walnut: Serve with a roast beetroot and rocket salad or with fresh pasta.

- Nasturtium and Pumpkin Seed: I serve this pesto on top of a chilled summer cucumber or courgette soup. I was inspired by the local city farm where there were huge beds of bright nasturtiums climbing all over at the end of summer.

NOTES
Nasturtiums are very easy to grow in a pot if you fancy. Just throw a packet of seeds in some compost in spring and they should provide you with spicy leaves and edible flowers all summer.

I started making harissa one year when the wild garlic was back, carpeting the local park, filling all the gaps with its bright vivid green and tempting me to harvest far more than I knew what to do with. I was looking for new ideas. This sauce has a rich depth and warmth to it. I have served it with fresh cheese on toast, folded through warm lentils with feta, drizzled over fried eggs or roast potatoes and garlic.

You can make it with coriander, parsley and rocket as the green base, but with wild garlic too, or experiment with any leaves and herbs you like.

Harissas

MAKES 200ml

- 1/2 tsp coriander seeds
- 1/2 tsp cumin seeds
- 1/2 tsp cardamom seeds
- 2 red or green chillies, deseeded and chopped
- 60g coriander
- juice of 1/4 lemon
- pinch of salt
- grind of pepper
- olive oil

WILD GARLIC
- 60g wild garlic

GREEN HERB
- 30g parsley
- 30g rocket

EQUIPMENT
- pestle and mortar
- small blender

Lightly toast all the seeds in a dry frying pan, then transfer them to a pestle and mortar and crush them to a fine powder. Set aside.

Place the chillies in a small blender, add the coriander, wild garlic or green herbs, lemon juice, salt and pepper, then add the crushed seeds to the blender and blitz everything together, gradually adding a stream of olive oil until you have a thick paste. Serve.

- Wild Garlic: Fold through lentils or drizzle over ricotta or feta salads.

- Green Herb: Serve with grilled lamb, BBQ pork or drizzled over fried eggs with yoghurt.

We took a trip to Istanbul a few years ago and just ate, drank, smelt interesting and delicious things the entire time. Grilled mackerel fillets folded in fresh bread from a man fishing and grilling by the river; sitting on the harbour on the Asian side eating sticky baklava watching huge cruise ships; hot, sweet milk flavoured with orchid root after a complicated ferry trip up the Bosphorus; amazing sesame flatbreads, grilled lamb, smoky aubergines and spiced yoghurt dips with grilled chicken and cooling yoghurt drinks on plastic stools in the spice market...

Yoghurts

Sweet Cumin

Place the yoghurt in a small bowl, add the olive oil, cumin and sugar and whisk together. Season with the salt and pepper. Serve with chicken tagine, or BBQ or roast lamb'.

MAKES 200ml

- 150g live full-fat natural yoghurt
- 1 tbsp extra virgin olive oil
- 1 heaped tsp ground cumin
- 1 heaped tsp caster sugar
- pinch of salt and pepper

Garlic and Lemon

Place the yoghurt in a small bowl, then whisk in the olive oil, garlic, lemon, salt and pepper. Serve as a dip with fresh bread and seasonal vegetables or with slow roast lamb or grilled fish.

MAKES 200ml

- 150g live full-fat natural yoghurt
- 1 tbsp extra virgin olive oil
- 1 garlic clove, peeled and grated
- zest and juice of 1/2 lemon
- pinch of salt and pepper

Smoky Aubergine

While the barbecue is heating up, place the aubergine on the grill and leave to char, turning it occasionally, gently pressing it flat as you do so, so it is blackened all over and soft all the way through. It needs to be completely collapsed, almost falling apart. Remove from the grill, cut it in half and leave to cool.

When the aubergine is cool enough to handle, scoop out all of the soft insides into a bowl, avoiding the black charred skin if you can. Chop the flesh finely, then add the yoghurt and lemon juice and mix with a fork. Serve with anything off the BBQ.

NOTES
Smaller aubergines are generally better for this dip as they won't be full of seeds.

MAKES 300ml

- 1 aubergine
- 200g live full-fat yoghurt
- squeeze of lemon juice

EQUIPMENT
- barbecue

In the beginning at Cook House I had lots of different salad dressings, but over time we have settled on a house dressing. We get so many compliments for it and people are constantly asking for the recipe.

People often tell us how good our salads are and that their own salads or the salads made by someone in their house are always disappointing. This is in large part down to the dressing. Read the salad section on page 62 for tips on balance and textures, which are very important, but once you have a good dressing ready in the fridge you are halfway there. All of these will keep for a few weeks refrigerated.

Dressings

Cook House

Whisk the mustard, vinegar, maple syrup and salt together in a bowl until completely smooth, then add the olive oil in a slow steady stream, whisking vigorously at the same time. It should start to emulsify into a thicker homogeneous dressing. Whisk harder if it doesn't! Alternatively, use a small blender.

MAKES 185ml

- 2 tsp Dijon mustard
- 3 tbsp white wine vinegar
- 2 tbsp maple syrup
- pinch of sea salt
- 100ml olive oil

Panzanella

Whisk the balsamic vinegar, salt, maple syrup, mustard and grated garlic together in a bowl until completely smooth, then add the olive oil in a slow steady stream, whisking vigorously at the same time. It should start to emulsify into a thicker homogeneous dressing. Whisk harder if it doesn't! Alternatively, use a small blender.

MAKES 180ml

- 2 tbsp balsamic vinegar
- 1/2 tsp sea salt
- 1 tbsp maple syrup
- 1 tbsp Dijon mustard
- 1/2 garlic clove, peeled and grated
- 120ml olive oil

Anchovy

Mix the anchovies, capers, grated garlic, vinegar, salt and pepper together in a bowl with a fork, then add the olive oil and mix.

MAKES 100ml

- 1 small 50g tin anchovies in olive oil, drained and chopped
- 1 tbsp capers
- 2 garlic cloves, peeled and grated
- 1 tbsp red wine vinegar
- salt and pepper
- 50ml olive oil

How To...

Set up a Restaurant in a Shipping Container

I have lost count of the amount of emails I have had from all over the world asking for tips and advice about this. People travel to see me to look at what we have done as they want to do something similar themselves.

01 **Find some land:** Ask around about empty plots of land in your neighbourhood – approach developers, car park owners and the council. My site belonged to the architects I used to work for and was staring me in the face for a while before I realized!

02 **Get permission:** We sketched out a design, then spoke to the planning department at the council. They were really helpful. You might need

someone to help you with the design of your development. An architect should be able to draw it up for you for the planning application.

03 **Get some shipping containers:** These are available online, varying wildly in price. You will need to hire a crane or HIAB truck to transport them when you are ready.

04 **Utilities:** You will need to think about where water, sewage, electric and gas are going to come from. This is also

something that should inform your choice of site. Get prices for these connections before you begin as it can be very costly.

05 **Design:** Think about how to configure your containers and where you will need holes cut; an architect can advise and you will also need a metal worker to do the cutting. We positioned the containers side by side then offset them and cut out the middle, creating a central space.

06 **Warmth:** How you are going to stay warm is a very important question. We insulated the walls and lined them with plywood. We installed a wood burner, which heated the space quickly, but very cold days required additional plug-in heaters.

07 **Further considerations:** create a welcoming and comfortable atmos-phere for your customers using internal lighting, furniture land-scaping, decoration and styling. Good luck!

Pay What You Feel

I found myself following a small circle of people doing interesting things in London: James Ramsden and The Young Turks who became The Clove Club, among others, were hosting small dinners in their houses or in other interesting small venues around the city, and more ideas started to form in the back of my mind.

I have never wanted to have strangers round to my house for a supper club – the thought of people nosing round, trekking upstairs to the loo or staying too long is just all too uncomfortable. I do not want to be in an episode of Come Dine With Me – no way. But the planning I had been putting into dinners for friends and family began to turn into ideas about a dinner for the public.

After a lot of notes, scribbles, thoughts and ideas I decided to just go for it. 'Come to a pop-up feast in a shipping container,' I tweeted and a day later twenty people had booked in to do just that. Who knew people were so keen to dine in a little metal box in the Ouseburn? A lot went into that evening: thinking about menus, styling and imagining who might actually want to come. Much of the menu was inspired by Joe Beef, a Montreal institution I'm determined to visit one day and also one of my favourite cookbooks – full of smörgåsbords, home smokers, oysters and sausage martinis, it's all right up my street.

My first supper club was about to become a reality. I didn't know what to charge people for the evening: who was I to ask for thirty or forty pounds? They didn't know if I could cook or if it would be any good. I didn't have any reputation, a booking system or any means of taking payment at this point, so I settled on an idea that I had heard about in a place in Berlin where guests were given an envelope at the end of the evening and asked to 'pay what you feel'. It was a risk, but I had tried to keep my costs as low as possible and it seemed like quite an exciting way to play it.

People began arriving just after seven – a few friends for moral support, but mainly strangers. There was a bit of polite chatter, which quickly grew in volume as guests settled in. Even at that early point in time, when it was just literally a box, there was a lovely atmosphere in the space. I have always enjoyed hanging out there: fire burning, music playing, hot toddies on hand.

We served a delicious cocktail of whisky, ginger ale, fresh lemon, orange, honey and cayenne pepper to warm the cold arrivals and it wasn't long before it was noisy and warm. My nerves lasted much longer than those of the guests. I was hugely anxious, probably until very near the end. I put it

down to it being the first event, but to be honest I still get nerves now; always incredibly tense until the main course has gone out, then I slowly begin to relax and see what a good thing we've put together.

The long table was laid ready with smörgåsbord starters as people sat down all together: home-made salami, pickled mackerel rollmops, sweet cucumber and horseradish crème fraîche with lavosh crackers, a dill and mustard potato salad, and my newest favourite discovery: Beer Cheese, a Joe Beef recipe that blends blue cheese, cottage cheese and cream cheese with hot beer, garlic and paprika.

There was no oven or equipment in the containers at this point so I cooked the pork at home slowly for nine hours and then had to send Adrian on a quick pork run back to the house; it was so soft, sticky and delicious, it just fell apart. I calmed down a little at that point – perhaps the glass of red wine helped. The pork was taken to the table alongside a secret recipe of baked beans, my own special barbecue sauce, creamy coleslaw with apple and toasted pumpkin seeds and fresh white home-baked buns.

Loud laughter and chatter filled the shipping container, the windows had steamed up and the woodburner was puffing out wood smoke and keeping us all very warm. Pudding was a collection of Campari and bitter orange jellies, warm pumpkin spice muffins and little chocolate and chestnut pots made

with melted chocolate, cream and chestnut purée, served with coffee and a splash more wine.

We opened the envelopes excitedly at the end. I found on this occasion (and into the future, as I used this method for quite a long time) that people generally left between twenty and thirty pounds. People were sometimes less or more generous, but it usually balanced out nicely. Once an envelope contained a hundred pounds; a few times there was nothing! One of the nicest things about the envelopes was the lovely messages people would write on them, showing real genuine warmth and thanks for the food, experience and new friends they had made. I still have a stack of them at home that I like to keep.

We ended the night dancing round the fire in the shipping container, watching kids throw fireworks into a burning bin over the other side of the valley and eating leftover pulled pork – a pretty lovely evening all in all.

SALADS

Salads

A good salad should have contrasting tastes, textures and temperatures. You should find different elements in the dish and be running your finger over the plate at the end to taste the last of all the mingled flavours. It is a world apart from undressed cold cucumber, tomato and lettuce on the side, which is what a lot of people consider to be a salad.

Your salad game will be strong if you are well prepared. Keep small jars of toasted seeds, nuts and toasted leftover bread made into breadcrumbs. Pestos, capers, pickles and dressings can all be made in advance and kept for months, and added to whatever fruit and vegetables you have to hand.

I use our Cook House Dressing (see page 53) for most of my salads. It is just the right balance of sharp, sweet and spice. I always dress the leaves first in a large bowl to make sure everything is coated in a light layer of dressing. Then I start to add the rest of the ingredients or build the salad up on the plate, thinking all the time about what exciting mouthfuls I'm putting together with the ingredients I have.

I have grown my own beetroot for a few years now, of which I'm always quite proud. Every time I pull a root vegetable out of the earth it amazes me that I actually grew it from the tiniest of seeds.

Combined with some cheese and my newest find, cooked grapes, this salad has it all going on. I started by throwing some grapes on the barbecue, then discovered that roasted in the oven and scattered through salads they are a delight. The grapes provide sweet bursts of flavour alongside earthy beetroot, toasted nuts, fresh mint and tangy goat's cheese.

Beetroot and Goat's Cheese Salad with Roast Grapes and Mint Pesto

SERVES 4 main, 6 side

- 500g beetroot
- 1 small bunch of black grapes
- splash of olive oil
- salt and pepper
- 30g toasted hazelnuts or seeds
- 250g salad leaves, such as spinach, rocket, pea shoots or Little Gem lettuce
- 1 quantity of Cook House Dressing (see page 53)
- 100g hard goat's cheese

PESTO
- 70g mint
- 60g toasted hazelnuts
- 35g Parmesan cheese
- 2 garlic cloves
- splash of red wine vinegar
- large glug of olive oil

EQUIPMENT
- toasting tray
- baking tray
- blender

Preheat the oven to 200°C/400°F/Gas 6. Place the beetroot on a roasting tray and roast for 40–60 minutes. They will take less time if they are young and fresh and more if they are large and old. You can tell they are done when a knife slides into them easily and the skin has started to harden and blister.

Meanwhile, pick the grapes from the stalks and place them on a small baking tray with the splash of olive oil and $1/4$ teaspoon salt and some pepper. Put them in the oven with the beetroot for 20 minutes until they have started to caramelize and brown. When they are done, leave to cool.

When the beetroot are done, remove from the oven, cover and leave to cool. When the beetroot are cool enough to handle, peel off the skins with the back of a knife and cut into bite-size pieces. Set aside.

To make the pesto, blitz the mint, hazelnuts, Parmesan, garlic, salt, pepper vinegar and the large glug of olive oil together in a blender, until smooth.

To assemble the salad, simply mix the beetroot with the pesto in a bowl; you might not need it all. Then add some toasted hazelnuts or seeds and throw in the roasted grapes.

In a separate bowl, dress the leaves with the dressing and pile these onto a plate. Gently arrange the beetroot, grapes and nuts on top. Finally, crumble the goat's cheese over the top of the salad and drizzle on a little more pesto.

This salad has found a permanent place on the Cook House menu. I think there would be a revolt if we were to remove it! I change this salad with the seasons, using shredded roast chicken and cubes of roast celeriac or squash in autumn and winter and making it fresh and light in spring and summer with poached chicken and raw spring vegetables.

Chicken, Courgette and Pea Salad with Aïoli and Sourdough Crumb

Place the chicken in a large pan and cover with cold water. Add the stock vegetables, bay leaf and peppercorns and bring to the boil, then reduce the heat so it is simmering very gently, the water should only just be moving. If you boil it too vigorously the chicken will be tough and dry out. Simmer for 45 minutes, or until the juices run clear when you pierce it with a knife. Remove the chicken from the pan and place it in a large tray to cool.

When the chicken is cool enough to handle, shred every last piece of meat off the bones and place in a large bowl. Add a few spoonfuls of the poaching stock with some salt and pepper and mix well. It should be moist and well seasoned.

To make the sourdough crumb, preheat the oven to 180°C/350°F/Gas 4. Blitz the leftover bread in a small food processor, tip it into a baking tray, add the olive oil and some salt and pepper and mix well with your hands. Put it in the oven for 20 minutes, or until golden brown, shaking the tray halfway through.

Then it's just a case of assembling your salad. Put the salad leaves into a large bowl, peel ribbons of courgette into the bowl using a vegetable peeler, and pod your peas straight in there too. Add 2 tablespoons of the dressing and mix well, then add a large handful of chicken per person to the salad and mix again.

Divide the salad among serving plates and serve topped with the sourdough crumb and a big dollop of Aïoli (see page 43) on the side.

SERVES 4

- 1 whole chicken
- stock vegetables: 1 onion, peeled and cut into quarters, 1 carrot, peeled and cut into quarters and 1 celery stick, cut into quarters
- 1 bay leaf
- 6 black peppercorns
- salt and pepper
- 2 slices of leftover bread, preferably sourdough
- 2 tbsp olive oil
- 1 large handful per person of mixed leaves, such as spinach, rocket, pea shoots or little gem lettuce
- 1 courgette
- 200g fresh peas in the pod
- 1 quantity of Cook House Dressing (see page 53)

EQUIPMENT
- food processor
- baking tray

NOTES

Reserve the chicken stock and freeze to use for soups, stews or risottos.

Courgettes are easy and fast to grow. I think if you sat and watched you could actually see it happen when they get going in midsummer. They say never to have more than one plant, but I always ignore that and grow four or five, then don't know what to do with them all. This salad is a good way of using up a glut. It is delicious, light and fresh with wafer-thin slices of courgette dressed in lemon and oil and crumbled creamy feta and fresh mint.

Courgette, Feta, Mint and Lemon Salad

To make the salad, shave the courgettes into wafer-thin ribbons with a vegetable peeler and place in a bowl. Add the olive oil, salt, pepper and lemon juice and mix together.

Scatter the courgettes onto a serving plate, then crumble the feta over the top and add the chopped mint and a few toasted pinenuts to bring some texture. Serve.

SERVES 2

- 2 courgettes
- 1 tbsp extra virgin olive oil
- salt and pepper
- juice of 1/4 lemon
- 50g feta cheese
- 1 handful of chopped mint
- few toasted pinenuts

This is one of my favourites when the first British asparagus lands in the shops in April – it's worth waiting until it does as the new season crop is always so delicious! I love black pudding too, and these guys like each other.

Black Pudding, Asparagus, Pea, Mint and Chunky Croûton Salad

SERVES 2

- splash of olive oil
- 200g Stornoway black pudding or similar (this one is my favourite), cut into cubes
- 2 slices of sourdough bread, cut into cubes
- 200g asparagus, woody ends snapped off and discarded and spears cut into 2.5-cm pieces
- 100g frozen or fresh peas
- 2 sprigs of mint, chopped, for topping

Add a splash of olive oil to a large non-stick frying pan and put it over a medium heat. Throw the black pudding and sourdough cubes into the pan and fry, stirring occasionally, until they start to brown and sizzle but not cooking too fast.

Throw the asparagus into the pan, then add the peas and cook until all the ingredients are hot and the juices have mingled. Serve on a warm plate topped with chopped mint.

London was awash with blood oranges in January. Margot Henderson drizzled them over an impressive looking cheesecake, the Clove Club served them with a delicious goat's curd and emerald green fennel granita, Quo Vadis had them with Campari and Spuntino in a sprightly salad with walnuts.

Instead of filling my bags with the wonders of Liberty's jewellery department, which I really wanted to do, I filled my handbag with blood oranges from a delightful little shop and brought them all the way back to Newcastle. The result was this simple, seasonal salad.

Blood Orange, Fennel, Walnut and Ricotta Salad

SERVES 2 lunch, 4 side

- 200g mixed bag of salad, such as watercress, spinach and rocket
- 1 tbsp extra virgin olive oil
- 1 tsp cider vinegar
- 1 tsp balsamic vinegar
- 1 tsp maple syrup
- salt and pepper
- 1 blood orange, peeled and thinly sliced
- 1 handful of walnuts
- 100g ricotta, crumbled

Alternatives

Feta

Place all the salad leaves in a bowl.

To make the dressing, mix the olive oil, both vinegars, maple syrup and salt and pepper together in a jam jar. Close the lid and shake to combine, then dress the leaves well.

Toast the walnuts in a dry frying pan, being careful that they don't burn. Mix the toasted walnuts and orange slices through the leaves. Pile the salad onto plates and finally top with some crumbled ricotta.

You can make this salad all year round depending on what's in season, but my favourite version is in autumn when there is so much bounty. It is a really hearty salad that is actually vegan served this way, but can also be topped with feta or goat's cheese if you like.

Autumnal Stale Bread Salad

Preheat the oven to 200°C/400°F/Gas 6. Toss all the root vegetables in olive oil with some salt and pepper, then place in a roasting tray and roast for 30 minutes, or until soft and golden. Remove from the oven and leave to cool.

Tear the bread into small chunks and splash with olive oil and salt and pepper. Rub the bread with your hands, then place on a baking tray and put into the oven with the vegetables for 10 minutes, or until golden, but not too rock hard!

Put the salad leaves in a large bowl and dress with the Panzanella Dressing. Add the apple and raw kale to the bowl and mix well.

Pile the salad onto plates and top gently with the roast vegetables, the sourdough croûtons and a sprinkle of poppy seeds.

NOTES
Use any squash you like in this dish, but Crown Prince is especially good.

SERVES 4

- 1 carrot, peeled and cut into 2-cm cubes
- 1/2 butternut squash or any squash, peeled, deseeded and cut into 2-cm cubes
- 1 beetroot, peeled and cut into 2-cm cubes
- 1 parsnip, peeled and cut into 2-cm cubes
- 30ml olive oil
- salt and pepper
- 2 slices of sourdough bread
- 1 handful per person of mixed salad leaves
- 1 quantity of Panzanella Dressing (see page 53)
- 1 Granny Smith apple, peeled, cored and thinly sliced
- 2 large cavolo nero or Russian kale leaves, thinly sliced
- 1 tsp poppy seeds

EQUIPMENT
- roasting tray
- baking tray

This salad was the best thing about last Christmas, I remember Lou and I taste-testing it and being wide-eyed with joy. I am a self-confessed Brussels sprout fan, and I know many of you feel very differently to me, but I have to say that even the haters have actually enjoyed this.

Brussels Sprout Salad with Curried Aïoli, Pickled Shallots and Walnuts

Mix the sugar and vinegar together in a bowl and stir to dissolve. Separate the pieces of shallot out and add to the vinegar and sugar mix in the bowl. Leave to stand, preferably for an hour.

Preheat the oven to 220°C/425°F/Gas 7. Arrange the sprouts in a large baking tray and coat with a little olive oil and some salt and pepper. Roast in the oven for 20 minutes, or until they start to take on some colour but haven't gone soggy!

Add the walnuts to another baking tray and put them in the oven with the sprouts for 10 minutes. Remove, cool, then break them up with your hands.

Spread a few large spoonfuls of the Curried Aïoli over the base of a serving plate. As soon as the sprouts are ready, add them to the plate in a big pile, then drizzle with more aïoli and top with the toasted walnuts, slivers of pickled shallot and lots of chopped dill.

SERVES 4

- 4 tbsp caster sugar
- 4 tbsp white wine vinegar
- 1 shallot, peeled and thinly sliced
- 500g Brussels sprouts, bases trimmed and cut in half
- 1 tbsp olive oil
- salt and pepper
- 1 quantity of Curried Aioli (see page 45)
- 1 handful of walnuts
- chopped dill, for sprinkling

EQUIPMENT

- baking trays

How To...

Start a Supper Club

My little restaurant started life six years ago as some hired tables and benches in an empty space when I decided I was ready to go beyond cooking for friends and family. After reading about and attending a few events in London I decided to take the plunge!

01 **Decide on a concept:** I based my first dinner around the cookbook of a restaurant in Montreal called Joe Beef. I was passionate about the food and menu, which was key.

02 **You need some guests:** I invited a few friends and asked everyone I knew to help spread the word online. I promoted it on my blog and social media. Think about your language making it sound as inviting, delicious and fun as possible.

03 **'Pay what you feel'?:** I took the risky strategy of letting my guests decide what they wanted to pay. You might be happier using a ticket site so guests have already paid up front. Work out your food costs and charge about four times this to cover utilities, hire or room dressing, staff costs, time, and hopefully a little profit.

04 **Put time and effort into your space:** make it inviting and comfortable. I hired tables and benches and

covered them with curtains repurposed as tablecloths. I lit candles in jars, hung white fabric to cover the unattractive walls and projected an animated puppet film on one. I designed and printed small menus with food illustrations and picked big boughs of berries and foliage to go in jars. I used a roll of greaseproof paper as a table runner, which looked great and was quite practical too!

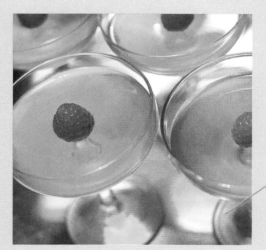

05 **Cook things you know and love.** My food was all seasonal and things I had tried out many times before. I think I spent about £5 per person in total. Design your menu so you can do as much as possible in advance.

06 **Booze:** Avoid complicated alcohol laws by making it bring-your-own.

07 **Things will go wrong:** You'll forget things, toilets will block and plates will fall, but you will improvise and have a good time: if everything goes well, or even if it doesn't, it is such a rewarding experience.

Architecture vs Food

I stuck with 'pay what you feel' for quite a few years. I found my events would sell out incredibly quickly, usually within twenty-four hours no matter what. People would read about the event, think: 'That looks good, interesting, different and exciting; I don't even have to part with cash, let's book!'

I put a lot of work into the wording and graphics, making everything sound delicious, beautiful and inviting. I had strong imagery and made sure I had beautiful photos taken from the start so I could encourage people to come to the next, and the next, and the next event. A combination of good design, enticing menus and appealing photography was definitely a factor in building up a solid reputation – and attracting faithful customers.

Tickets would literally fly out as soon as I put them on sale. I would get hundreds of requests for the twenty slots available. I started with a first-come-first-served system, but very often it was the same people who were incredibly quick off the mark, so I started to just leave the booking window open for twenty-four hours, then pick names at random. I was careful not to run events too often; I was working a full-time job as well, so this suited me regardless, but I wanted the supper clubs to seem exciting and unique at the same time, so that people were dying to attend the next one. It is a finely nuanced thing I think, and a combination of hard work, attention to detail and being in the right place at the right time.

I still hold private party supper clubs where people hire the whole place, but the original mixed events with a bunch of strangers will always be my true love and I try to keep aspects of them in everything I do. I love seeing people arrive, nervously; sometimes some of the party haven't even been told it is a long table event, where you will have to talk to people next to you. I remember clearly the look of horror on one man's face as he came through the door and realised this, but he left happy, and a bit drunk...

I have always paid huge attention to the details of making people feel comfortable and at home, knowing that this communal dining style is not something that comes naturally to the British: light levels, music levels, talking points on the table, sharing food to encourage family-style behaviour, generosity in food portions and a warm welcome. I love what I do for the hospitality and conviviality as much as I do the food.

Seeing people leave, hugging other guests goodbye whom they have never met before; hugging me, with huge smiles, having had a lovely time; that's what I got into this for. It is totally heart-warming and I love it.

Not long after I started hosting these dinners, a man from the National

Trust rang me, and said he'd heard about what I was up to – could they come along to one of my dinners? Two of them drove down from Seahouses in Northumberland to attend the next event. They loved it, and from that came about an exciting partnership that spanned three summers. We hosted dinners in Lindisfarne Castle and on the Farne Islands, a group of islands which is also a bird sanctuary, a mile out to sea off the Northumberland Coast.

The logistics of these events were some of the hardest things I have ever done, but they were also some of the greatest experiences of my life. I remember one day so clearly: I had been over to the Farnes to host a lunch in the fourteenth-century chapel on the island. I did it on my own, which was incredibly stupid. I planned, cooked, packed, lifted and served every last detail single-handed. We're talking flowers, glasses, tablecloths, ice, vases, cake stands – everything. It was a lovely menu of rabbit terrine, pickles, tiny caramelized garlic tarts, wild garlic devilled eggs, homemade butter, breads, pork pies with apple relish, lovely spring salads with peas and shoots, homemade lemonade and strawberries and meringues. The guests loved it.

It was a beautiful sunny day and after packing every last thing back up into my huge waterproof boxes we got the boat home, the sun glinting on the water, seabirds diving around us, spray in the air; we were suddenly joined by four dolphins who swam along with the boat as we made our way back to the harbour, leaping out of the water and racing around the bow of the boat. I sat on the harbour wall in the sun when I got back and thought I actually couldn't be happier; what a lovely day, an amazing setting for lunch, all the food turned out beautifully, the guests loved it and then that... a magical sunny boat ride with dolphins leading the way. It was amazing.

I went back to the Farnes to serve dinner on a few evenings that summer. We plucked lobsters straight from the sea, cooked them in seawater and set up a makeshift kitchen in the island's Pele Tower, which was a bit of a challenge. The guests watched whales and dolphins swim past as they had drinks at the top of the island, and we got attacked by irate terns as we tried to ferry food across the courtyard where they nested.

On one occasion the weather was warm enough to dine outside at Lindisfarne Castle; it was a pretty magical evening. From the castle you can see all the way up the coast to Scotland and all the way down Northumberland. You can hear seals calling on the wind and look down over Holy Island eating lobster, langoustines and flowers and herbs from the Gertrude Jekyll garden.

Place has always been important to me, and setting is essential to lots of different things I do – whether that's a dinner at Cook House, or in a castle or a wild valley. It isn't just window dressing for photos, it is as important as the eating and the whole experience. Thinking about those details brings real joy into people's lives.

For the next two and a half years I continued to work in this way, full time in architecture, and then taking my holidays to host pop-up supper clubs in the containers, in castles, on islands, in railway sheds, pubs, wine shops... I saw spaces I loved and started planning, and people began to approach me too.

I loved it, but it was exhausting and stressful. I was basically doing two jobs at the same time and one of them I was making up as I went along; or perhaps that was both of them? Either way, it was a lot of pressure, but I had begun to recognize that this is what I wanted to do.

With hindsight I have realised that the relationship between food and architecture is closer than I first thought. People refer to me wildly changing path and starting an entirely different career, but I think there are many transferable skills between the professions. Architecture is about people and good architects think about the people, not themselves. I think attention to people's behaviour, how they use space; making people feel comfortable; the right light, warmth and acoustics: all these make people feel at ease whether it is in a school, an office or your home.

Transfer that to running a restaurant and it is all of those ideas on a smaller scale. I still think about all those things I have learnt. Atmosphere and the setting you create is equally as important as what is served on your plate, and it's in that that the two professions tie together, I think.

Bringing someone a plate of food is also so much more immediate than architecture, which is something I love. Four years' blood, sweat and tears working on a building where you hate the sight of it and everyone involved by the end was not my joy.

ON
TOAST

On Toast

My go-to easy midweek dinner is 'things on toast' and there is usually at least one thing on the menu at Cook House on toast too. Because a) who doesn't love toast and b) it's easy. Which doesn't mean it can't also be delicious and interesting.

A dinner of two pieces of buttered toast with two toppings is my ideal. One might be eggs and chorizo, or lemony, garlic courgettes, or ricotta, honey and rocket; the other could be bacon, broad beans and parsley or black pudding and mint, or duck hearts, chorizo and chestnuts. There are usually some scraps in the fridge that can stretch to become a toast topping.

Use nice large slices of sourdough and lots of butter too.

I have a vivid memory of a plate of sliced tomatoes with olive oil and an obscene amount of diced garlic in southern Spain; it was one of the most delicious things I've ever eaten. Tomatoes in this country never really live up to the standards of a plate of fresh tomatoes in Spain or Italy, but roasting can bring out the best in them. These sweet and rich flavours mingling with the fresh cheese and sinking into your toast make a delicious late summer lunch.

Roast Tomatoes, Ricotta and Mint

SERVES 2

- 200g cherry tomatoes on the vine
- 2 garlic cloves, peeled and crushed
- splash of olive oil
- salt and pepper
- 2 thick slices of sourdough bread
- good-quality extra virgin olive oil, for drizzling
- 200g ricotta
- 2 sprigs of mint, chopped
- 1 tsp nigella seeds

EQUIPMENT
- baking tray

Preheat the oven to 200°C/400°F/Gas 6. Leave the tomatoes on the vine and place on a baking tray with the crushed garlic, a splash of olive oil and some salt and pepper. Roast for 25 minutes, or until the tomatoes have started to form brown blisters and the liquid in the bottom of the tray is turning sticky rather than watery.

Toast the sourdough bread, then drizzle one side with extra virgin olive oil and spread a good centimetre-thick layer of ricotta on top. Remove the tomatoes from the vine and scatter them over the top of the ricotta. You can add the roasted crushed garlic and the pan juices too.

Top with the chopped mint, a sprinkle of nigella seeds, lots of pepper and a drizzle of extra virgin olive oil.

I watch people order this in the garden at Cook House on a sunny summer's day and feel really pleased for them. It is a very simple dish but utterly delicious: soft eggs, loads of herbs and fresh mayonnaise with a hint of heat and sweetness. A friend gave me the recipe knowing I was an egg mayonnaise fan and I've served it ever since.

Soft Egg and Herb Tartine

Place the egg and egg yolk in a small bowl with the Dijon mustard, the vinegar and a pinch of salt and, using a hand-held blender, blend until smooth. Add the olive oil, a little at a time, blending as you go to make a mayonnaise. Keep adding oil until it has begun to thicken: you want it to be the consistency of yoghurt. Add the remaining mustard, the yoghurt, honey and some pepper, then add the herbs and blitz until the herbs are chopped.

Scrape the mayonnaise into a bowl using a spatula and taste, adding more honey, salt or mustard if needed. Add the capers and stir through.

To cook the eggs, bring a pan of salted water to the boil, lower in the eggs gently and boil for 6 1/2 minutes. Remove the eggs and run under cold water to cool and stop them cooking.

To serve, shell the eggs and slice in half on top of some hot sourdough toast. Drizzle the sauce over generously, then top with more dill, mint and tarragon, some extra virgin olive oil and lots of pepper.

SERVES 2

SAUCE
- 1 whole egg
- 1 egg yolk
- 2 tsp Dijon mustard
- 1 tsp white wine vinegar
- salt and pepper
- 150ml olive oil
- live full-fat natural yoghurt
- 1 tbsp honey
- 1 handful of dill, plus extra for sprinkling
- 1 handful of mint, plus extra for sprinkling
- 1 handful of tarragon, plus extra for sprinkling
- 2 tbsp baby capers

TOAST
- 4 large eggs
- 4 slices of hot sourdough toast
- extra virgin olive, for drizzling

EQUIPMENT
- small hand-held blender

A day out in search of mushrooms is an incredibly enjoyable day in my book. Wandering through beautiful sunny woodland, silence and birdsong, excitedly spotting tiny fungi poking through the leaves, filling your bags, to return home and eat delicious earthy, buttery, garlicky mushrooms on toast. Make sure you only cook those you are 100 per cent sure are safe to eat.

Garlic Wild Mushrooms

Melt a generous amount of butter in a large frying pan with a splash of oil to stop it burning, over a medium heat. When the butter is hot and melted, throw in the mushrooms and swirl them round until they're coated in the butter. Fry for about 5 minutes, allowing them to take on some colour as they cook.

When the mushrooms look golden, add the grated garlic and cook for another 30 seconds, then scrape everything out of the pan onto the buttered toast. Top with a sprinkle of chopped parsley and serve.

NOTES

Clean the mushrooms using a small brush, paintbrush or toothbrush if you don't have a mushroom brush, brushing away any soil, sand or leaves.

SERVES 2

- 25g butter
- 1 tbsp olive oil
- 200g hedgehog, cep or chanterelle mushrooms, cleaned and chopped into even-sized pieces
- 1 garlic clove, peeled and grated
- 2 slices of sourdough bread, toasted and buttered
- 1 tsp chopped flat leaf parsley

I had read about the Shooter's Sandwich previously in Elizabeth David's *Summer Cooking*. 'The wise' she says, 'travel with a flask of whiskey and a Shooter's Sandwich. With this sandwich a man may travel from Land's End to Quaker Oats, and snap his fingers at both.' We didn't go quite that far, but we did take it on a picnic in the Lake District in December on one of the stormiest days of the year...

This is a serious sandwich! The mushroom mix is so tasty with rich meat and sharp hot horseradish and mustard. Make a day ahead of serving becuase it needs to be pressed overnight for best results.

Shooter's Sandwich

SERVES 6

- 1 large round crusty loaf
- 50g butter
- 500g large field mushrooms or fresh wild mushrooms if you have access, cleaned and finely chopped
- 200g shallots, peeled and finely chopped
- salt and pepper
- 2 garlic cloves, peeled and grated
- 1 tbsp brandy
- 1 tsp Worcestershire sauce
- 2 rib-eye steaks, about 200g and 2cm thick
- 1 tbsp Dijon mustard
- 1 tbsp horseradish cream

EQUIPMENT
- string

Alternatives
Roasted vegetables

Slice a 'lid' off the top of the loaf and hollow out the centre. You can keep the middle and freeze it to use for breadcrumbs at some point. Melt the butter in a frying pan and then sweat the mushrooms and shallots over a medium heat until they are tasty and soft and have lost most of their moisture. Season with salt and pepper, then add the grated garlic, brandy and Worcestershire sauce.

Season the steaks generously with salt and pepper on both sides. Heat a frying pan until very hot, add the steaks and cook for 11/2 minutes on each side for rare, or a touch more if you want them to be medium rare.

Quickly assemble the sandwich, no resting required. Spread the base of the loaf with the Dijon mustard, then put the first steak into the bottom of the loaf and add the mushroom and shallot mix, packing it into all the nooks and crannies. Place the next steak on top. Spread the top of this steak with horseradish and spread the inside of the loaf lid with a touch more. Pop the lid back on and wrap the whole loaf tightly in greaseproof paper. Secure with four lengths of string, as if you were tying up a parcel. Finally, place the loaf between two boards and place some heavy pans or weights on top. Leave to press overnight.

Cut the loaf into 6 wedges, still in its paper, and serve with some piccalilli or a good mustard; it's delicious!

We have had this mackerel pâté on and off the menu at Cook House from the beginning. I often take it off the menu thinking it is quite boring, but people always rave about it. Feeling lazy the other week I bought a ready-made pot from a high-end supermarket, and now I see why; it was really quite disgusting. This is so easy, delicious and so far removed from the shop mush.

Smoked Mackerel Pâté with Pickled Fennel

Remove the skin from the mackerel fillets and discard. Flake the fish into a large bowl, trying to pick out any bones as you go. Have a sift through it afterwards to look for any you have missed. Add the cream cheese, crème fraîche, lemon juice and horseradish and beat together with a fork.

Pack the mixture tightly into a ceramic pot or Tupperware container, trying to avoid any air bubbles, then seal the top with clingfilm. It will keep in the fridge for five days or until you are ready to use it. Serve on hot buttered toast with some pickled fennel (see page 293) and a green salad with lots of fresh mint.

NOTES

If you can't find fresh horseradish it is still very tasty without. And if you do ever find some, then peel it, cut it into smaller pieces and freeze it. It keeps well and you can grate it from frozen.

SERVES 6

- 1 pack of smoked peppered mackerel fillets, about 300g
- 150g full-fat cream cheese
- 100g full-fat crème fraîche
- juice of 1/4 lemon
- 3 tbsp grated fresh horseradish

EQUIPMENT

- ceramic pot or Tupperware container

Come autumn I am often inundated with birds from the shoot my dad attends, so one year as a thank you I potted up some pheasant for the proprietor and the keepers.

The best way to eat this potted pheasant is slightly warmed through, or at room temperature, on hot toast with butter and a scattering of capers. It's so delicious, the meat is soft and tender and smoky, the thyme and butter really add to the flavours. It's changed my view of pheasant no end...

Juniper and Wood-smoked Potted Pheasant

I smoke the pheasant in a smoker for 2 hours with a mix of hickory and apple wood and some juniper berries. If you don't have a smoker, preheat the oven to 200°C/400°F/Gas 6 and just roast the pheasant for 15 minutes instead.

When the pheasant is smoked or roasted, remove the legs and thighs and, using a pair of sharp scissors or game shears, cut the carcass in half lengthways and then in half again.

Preheat the oven to 150°C/300°F/Gas 2. To confit, put the jointed pheasant in a pot that it fits snugly in and pour over the warm duck or goose fat. You want the fat to cover the pheasant as much as possible. Add the bay leaf and thyme, then cook in the oven for 1–11/2 hours until the meat is soft and falling off the bone.

When it is done, take the pheasant out of the fat and leave to cool. You can keep the fat in a jar in the fridge and use again. Just reserve a little of the warm fat to mix through the meat and to pour over the top of the finished pheasant.

Shred the pheasant meat into tiny pieces; this is best done by hand so you can discard any bits of bone, skin or fat, and you get a nice irregular coarse texture rather than a pâté texture if you blitz it. Add a little of the melted fat occasionally to keep it from drying out. Add quite a few thyme leaves and some black pepper.

Melt the butter in a pan over a low heat. Add the lemon juice to the butter, then mix through the meat.

Pack the meat into sterilized jars or small pots and pour over a thin layer of the melted fat, just enough to cover. This will keep for a few months in the fridge. I find that one bird makes two 225g jars of potted pheasant.

MAKES 2 x 225g jars

- 1 whole plucked pheasant
- 350g duck or goose fat, warmed
- 1 bay leaf
- 1 bunch of thyme, plus extra thyme leaves
- pepper
- 25g butter
- juice of 1/2 lemon

EQUIPMENT
- smoker (optional)
- mix of hickory and apple wood and juniper berries (optional)
- sharp scissors or game shears
- sterilized jars or small pots

Alternatives
Duck; rabbit; pork

You see chicken liver pâté everywhere but my expectations are high – I want really high levels of butter and really pink soft tasty livers, so I started to make my own. I have often served this at supper clubs as you can make it well in advance, then if you seal the top with a thick layer of butter it keeps for a long time. Buy the best chicken livers you can, free-range and organic; they are cheap and you can tell the difference.

Potted Chicken Livers

Check over the chicken livers and snip out the tubes in the middle, gristle or anything that is green or not liver-coloured with a pair of scissors.

Melt 25g of the butter in a pan until sizzling, then add the livers and cook gently for 5 minutes, turning them constantly until they look cooked on the outside. When they are browned, remove the livers from the pan with a slotted spoon and place in a bowl.

Add the brandy and Madeira to the pan. Increase the heat briefly and let the alcohol burn off. Add the garlic and thyme to the chicken livers, then pour the boozy butter into the bowl and 30g of the remaining butter, then dice and pound the mixture. I use the pestle from my pestle and mortar. You are aiming to break down the livers but not remove all the texture. When it is all mixed and the butter has melted, season with salt and pepper then pour the mixture into ceramic ramekins or storage containers.

Melt the remaining 50g butter in a small pan, then pour it over the top to seal the livers. Serve with hot toast and a sweet pickle.

SERVES 6

- 300g fresh chicken livers
- 105g butter
- 1 tbsp brandy
- 1 tbsp Madeira
- 1/2 garlic clove, peeled and grated
- 1 large sprig of thyme
- salt and pepper

EQUIPMENT

- sterilized ceramic ramekins or storage containers

This salty feta whisked up with thick creamy yoghurt and bitter good-quality olive oil is a delicious vehicle for any number of toppings. You will need an open fire for the leeks, but if you don't have one this recipe works well with any number of different toppings. I've had it on and off the menu at Cook House in a huge number of different guises, including grilled peach and mint or roasted red peppers with rosemary...but this was one of the first variations I came up with and is still a favourite.

Whipped Feta with Smoked Leeks and Black Sesame

SERVES 6

WHIPPED FETA
- 200g block of feta
- 50g good-quality live full-fat natural yoghurt
- 30ml extra virgin olive oil

SMOKED LEEKS
- 3 leeks, trimmed
- salt
- 6 slices of sourdough bread
- toasted black sesame seeds, for sprinkling

EQUIPMENT
- stand mixer or hand whisk
- heatproof tongs

Crumble the feta into a bowl and add the yoghurt and olive oil. Either transfer the mixture to a stand mixer and whisk on high for 5 minutes, or use a hand whisk. There will still be some tiny lumps of feta, but in general the mix should become lighter, smoother and more aerated. Chill for an hour or so before using.

Push a couple of large leeks into the flames of a fire, so the whole of the white end and most of the green is engulfed by the heat and flames, leaving the leafy end poking out so you can get hold of it to turn. You can do this in a woodburner, an open fire or if you're having a barbecue push them into the coals. They will take about 15 minutes, turning occasionally. The whole of the outside will go black and charred. You will know that they are done as when you pick them up, with long heatproof tongs, they will collapse and bend as the inside is cooked and super soft, with juices sizzling into the fire.

Take them out, put them into a baking tray, cover with clingfilm and leave to cool. This also allows the smoky flavours to sink in. When they are cool enough to handle, remove the black outer layers. It's a messy job. You will be left with the soft cooked inner part of the leek that is lightly smoked and sweet in flavour. Shred this into a tangle and dress with a little olive oil and salt. It doesn't matter if you get the odd black bit here and there, I think it's unavoidable really.

To assemble, toast some sourdough bread, then spread with the feta mix, a good centimetre thick, and top with a tangled pile of smoked leeks and a sprinkle of toasted black sesame seeds. It's delicious – salty, smoky, sweet and nutty, a really good balance.

How To...
Plant an Edible Garden

I have a tiny strip of north-facing garden along the front of my house, but have made use of it so I no longer buy packs of herbs in the supermarket that inevitably collapse into a brown mush long before they are all used up. Even living in the North of England you can create a small edible garden that looks after itself.

01 **Dig over whatever soil you have** or buy some large pots and fill them with compost.

02 **Try planting from seed;** you just need small seed trays that you can put on a sunny windowsill. Plant the seeds according to the packet instructions, into damp soil and wait. It can be incredibly rewarding.

03 **Alternatively, you can buy plants** from a garden centre. I have bought quite a few unusual herbs from

National Trust properties, including hyssop and salad burnet.

04 **Plant them out in early spring,** when frosts have passed. I have planted mine quite densely, which removes the need for any weeding once they are established.

05 **Plant hardy herbs,** such as rosemary, lavender, thyme, tarragon, sage and mint. I plant nasturtium seeds direct into the ground in early spring and they

 trail around the other plants with bright splashes of orange and red. Marigolds, cornflowers and pansies all add colour and are edible too.

06 **Put in some sweet pea seedlings** if you have anywhere you can grow things upwards, a fence perhaps: they smell and look beautiful.

07 **You can attach vertical planters** to a fence to grow strawberries, squash or courgettes. French or runner beans will grow up a fence or against three

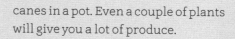

canes in a pot. Even a couple of plants will give you a lot of produce.

08 **A big pot of compost sowed with mixed salad seeds** is a great addition to your kitchen garden. It saves you buying salad that will go off before you finish it. Rocket, lambs lettuce, watercress, spinach, little gem and frisée will all improve your salad bowls no end. Carrots, beetroot or potatoes will all grow in a pot about 30cm deep, and take very little looking after.

Light Bulb Moments

As it happened, while I was trying to think of somewhere to set up an inexpensive, interesting restaurant, the answer was staring me straight in the face.

It was a conversation Adrian and I had regularly, about the restaurant that we would open one day. I would draw up small business plans, example menus, prices, staff rotas, do some sums and declare that it would work. It's a process I still enjoy now.

Early on in the daydream we even went to view a restaurant at the end of my street. It was on the market for a fairly reasonable amount of money for the area, which is a busy suburb five minutes from Newcastle city centre. I looked round with an agent; at the little kitchen, the yard that I imagined a little smoker puffing away in and herbs growing up the walls, a big basement for storage, a little dining room and street-side seats as well. It was cute. I could imagine it as a neighbourhood bistro, friendly, busy, serving tasty food and fun.

I can't remember how on earth I thought I was going to pay for it – I didn't have any money. My monthly salary only just covered my living expenses. So I'm not really sure what I was doing! Apart from exploring the dream, which I guess is as good a place as any to begin. It makes me laugh a bit now, however: I was playing make-believe, but I just wanted it to happen so much.

Afterwards the agent rang to see if I wanted to proceed and suggested other places to look at, and I had to decline as reality kept getting in the way. I continued to check the market for the next couple of years, always looking at what was out there, waiting for something miraculously cheap and interesting to appear – suffice to say nothing came about.

Early on, when this whole adventure was just a seed of an idea, I read a quote in the *Mission Street Food* book that said: 'You simply have to provide something that is more desirable than what is currently being offered. In many cases, this is as easy as it sounds,' and I thought *Yes, I can do that...*

We were in London in February 2014. I always try to go down as often as time and finances allow, to see friends and exhibitions, but really just to eat in as many interesting places as possible. I'll map out everywhere I want to eat, old favourites and new openings, and then agonise over whittling the list

down to something affordable and realistic for the couple of nights we end up staying. I love Newcastle and there is a good growing food scene in our relatively small city, but London is just bountiful in comparison.

We were walking to Rochelle Canteen to have lunch. I hadn't been before but had observed the place with interest, as it was exactly what I felt I wanted to achieve if my plans ever came together. Margot Henderson had long been a hero of mine; setting up the dining room above the French House, originally, and then Rochelle Canteen, I felt like she made her own rules.

Margot and Melanie, or Arnold & Henderson as they are known, run a small canteen that serves breakfast and lunch but also hosts all the best events, dinners and parties. Beautiful seasonal dishes in a very relaxed converted bike shed in the grounds of a Victorian school. It was everything I dreamt of, and clever too, in that it afforded everyone who worked there a quality of life and time out of the kitchen that's rare in the hospitality industry. It seemed achievable and enjoyable as a business model, albeit involving massive amounts of work.

I digress; we were off there for lunch, I was a fan, and wanted to actually experience the place – and to eat a lot, obviously.

On Shoreditch High Street, mid-conversation, Adrian suddenly said, 'Why don't you open a restaurant in the shipping containers?' There was a pause while we both took it in and processed it through the 'another ridiculous and unrealistic idea' filter, but I just thought, *Yes. That's exactly what we should do.* He's often right.

Over lunch we talked it through. It seemed so obvious and simple once we got thinking. Over the next few days in London we talked excitedly about nothing else: from a grand plan down to finer details, and the more we discussed it the more realistic it actually seemed. Was this one really going to happen?

We returned home and I was full of excitement about my new plans. Unlike in the past, this one wasn't going away. The more I planned and thought about it, the more I couldn't find any reason why I couldn't do it.

I asked to speak to my boss. I was nervous but at the same time so sure. I explained how I felt, that I wanted to leave and felt architecture was not my calling, something I'm sure he was well aware of; then went straight into the second half of my plan: how I wanted to rent the shipping containers from him. And that was it. I showed him a small business plan and he came back a few days later with a rental agreement and it was real! That was February and I worked as an architect until the end of April. My last day wasn't sad –

I literally did not look back. For a long time I didn't even want to go back into the building; I felt free of something I hadn't enjoyed for so long, and I wasn't going to mourn it for a second.

I named my business plan 'what would Margot do?' and set about realistically planning it all out. Because it was such a small space, we decided I could just run it myself to begin with. This alleviated a lot of my fears, as I was much less scared of taking it all on myself than of employing people, teaching people and relying on people. I wasn't quite there yet.

Monday to Friday I would serve breakfast and lunch. A small simple-to-serve offering for breakfast – home-made granola, stewed fruit, yoghurt, toast – that would allow me to prepare a small lunch menu at the same time, with lunch offering five or six simple, delicious and fresh dishes each day, such as salads, tarts, terrines and pâtés, I could get my head round it and saw it as a realistic plan. I planned to buy minimal and cheap domestic equipment and go from there.

My overheads were incredibly low, so the risk mentally and financially was also low. Staff costs were just myself, rent was low; the place was tiny so fell under the threshold for business rates; waste was minimal so collection costs were also minimal, and utilities again weren't too expensive as the place was so small.

MEAT & GAME

Meat & Game

A lot of the following recipes are big centrepieces for summer or winter, which are perfect for a gang of friends and family to tuck into. They are derived from my supper club menus or one-off dinners and are surrounded by fond memories of long tables, clinking glasses and happy faces.

These dishes are all big meat-based feasts, where it is worth the time to look for the best meat you can afford. Outdoor, free-range animals that have led a happy life will taste better on your palate and your conscience. I find myself thinking more and more about where my meat comes from and how much of it I choose to eat over the last few years. I prefer to seek out a good butcher and know where the animal has come from and how it has been raised. This isn't always possible so if I don't have time or I'm not sure, I'm very happy to cook and eat vegetables, pulses, eggs, cheese and all other food groups instead! I feel strongly that we should be responsible for our choices. I don't want to play a part in caged chickens or pigs that have never seen the sky. Do ask questions about your meat, spend a bit more but eat less and you will reap the reward.

It is not just a question of morals, the difference in quality shines through in the taste. People comment so often about our chicken at Cook House, about how amazing it tastes, how chicken-y it is, and ask what we have done to it – we have bought a big, fat, slow-grown, outdoor, free-range chicken that has had a nice life. Obviously, it is more expensive but so worth it.

In the winter we roast a chicken every day at Cook House and I have to stop myself from eating the oysters, wings, and those bits of skin round the edge of the cavity that get really crispy...

This recipe stuffs the space between the skin and the meat with a herby crème fraîche, which then melts into the chicken and mingles with all the juices when you carve it. You'll never look back.

Roast Chicken Stuffed with Crème Fraîche and Lovage

Preheat the oven to 220°C/425°F/Gas 7.

In a bowl, mix the lovage through the crème fraîche with a pinch of salt and pepper. With the cavity facing towards you, gently pull the chicken skin up and away from the breast meat, and start to separate the two with your finger, aiming to create a pocket which you can stuff with the crème fraîche mix. Open it up as far towards the back of the bird as you can, trying to not rip the skin. Spoon in the crème fraîche, pushing it back under the skin as you go, then place the thin slices of butter over the top of the chicken. Place the onion half inside the cavity. Squeeze the lemon juice over the chicken, then tuck the squeezed lemon into the cavity as well. Sprinkle the whole bird with salt and pepper.

Put the chicken in the oven for 20 minutes, then remove it from the oven, tip the chicken towards you so any juices in the cavity run into the tray and baste the bird in the juicy buttery mix all over the skin.

Put the chicken back into the oven, reducing the oven temperature to 190°C/375°F/Gas 5 and roast for another 40 minutes. Halfway through roasting, remove the chicken again and baste the skin with the juices. To check that the chicken is cooked, pierce the breast meat and between the leg and the breast with a skewer and if the juices run clear then the chicken is cooked. If not, pop it back in for another 10 minutes. Leave the chicken to rest for 15 minutes before carving.

SERVES 4–6

- 1 handful of lovage or another herb of choice, chopped
- 3 tbsp full-fat crème fraîche
- salt and pepper
- 1 large chicken
- 50g butter, thinly sliced
- 1/2 onion1/2 lemon

Alternatives

tarragon; thyme; sage

My dad is so obsessed with this pie – he gets a glazed look when he talks about it...'the Grazer chicken pie' he calls it, after my recipe website 'The Grazer'. If you're tired after a long week and want to cosy up on the sofa with dinner, this is so warming and comforting, it's my favourite thing on a Sunday night. The poached chicken is soft and juicy in a rich creamy sauce with buttery onions, smoky bacon and little sharp capers all topped with flaky pastry.

Chicken, Bacon and Caper Pie

SERVES 6

- 1 whole chicken
- 1 leek, trimmed and sliced
- 4 garlic cloves, peeled
- 3 onions, peeled;
  1 onion, chopped and
  the remaining 2 cut into
  chunky rounds
- few black peppercorns
- 45g butter
- about 5 streaky bacon
  rashers, chopped
- salt and pepper
- 1 handful of plain flour
- 800–900ml whole milk
- 1 large handful of capers
- 1 sheet of shop-bought
  puff or shortcrust pastry
- 1 egg, beaten

EQUIPMENT
- pie dish, 20x30cm
  approx

Put the chicken in a large pot with the leek, garlic, chopped onion and peppercorns. Fill the pan with cold water and bring to the boil, then reduce the heat and simmer very gently for 45 minutes, or until cooked. Remove the chicken from the pan and place on a tray to cool slightly. Reserve some of the poaching stock for the sauce.

Meanwhile, melt 20g of the butter in a frying pan and sweat the chunky onion rounds gently over a low heat for 30 minutes, or until meltingly soft. Remove the onions from the pan and set aside, then add the bacon and fry until golden and crispy. Set aside.

Preheat the oven to 190°C/375°F/Gas 5.

When the chicken is cool enough to handle, shred the meat from the bone into bite-size chunks. Mingle the chicken, all the onions and bacon together in a pie dish and season with salt and pepper.

Next, make the white sauce. Melt the remaining butter in a saucepan over a low heat, add the flour and whisk for a few minutes, allowing it to cook through a little, until it smells biscuit-y. Then start to whisk in the milk. It will thicken up very quickly to start with, but just keep whisking and adding the milk in a steady stream, a little at a time, letting it heat through as you do so as it will continue to thicken as it gets hot. When you have added all the milk, add a couple of ladles of the chicken stock and leave to heat up for 5 minutes. You're aiming for a silky creamy sauce, about the thickness of double cream. Finally, season to taste with salt and pepper.

Add the capers to the chicken mix, then pour the sauce over the chicken, bacon and onions and mix gently until everything is coated.

Unroll the pastry on a clean work surface. Depending on the size of your pie dish you may need to roll it out a little more. Beat the egg in a dish, then brush a little all round the edge of the pie dish. Carefully place the pastry over the dish and press down around the edges. Trim the excess pastry from around the edges of the dish, then, using a fork, press down all round the edges. You can use any excess pastry to make pie decorations. I like little leaves and berries or even initials for a personalised pie. Place them on top, then brush the top with more of the beaten egg for a lovely golden pastry crust. Cut a cross in the centre of the pastry to allow air to escape while it cooks and to stop the pastry getting soggy in the middle.

Bake in the oven for 30–40 minutes, until golden brown, then leave to rest for 10 minutes before you dig in.

NOTES

Keep the stock for soups, stews or sauces – it's so delicious and freezes really well.

Try to find extra-fine capers for the pie filling.

If you have a pie bird you can put it in before you drape the pastry over, instead of cutting a hole in the middle. They do the same job of allowing steam to escape while the pie bakes. My pie bird is called Peter.

A cassoulet is a stew of sorts, a rich slow-cooked French casserole, with roast or confit duck, sausages, bacon, a lovely stock full of herbs, tomatoes and lots of white beans, all topped with crispy, golden baked breadcrumbs. In the French peasant origins of the dish they used to deglaze the pot from the previous cassoulet as a base for the next one, and so on and so on, which led to stories of hundred-year-old cassoulets. This version is based around Elizabeth David's advice and is so delicious. It also produces plenty of leftovers and is good reheated with additional cooked sausages, or just served with crusty bread. It is rich and meaty and is one of my favourite things I have cooked.

Confit Duck Cassoulet with Sourdough Crumb

SERVES 4+

- splash of olive oil
- 2 onions, peeled and thinly sliced
- 6 rashers of smoked streaky bacon, chopped
- 500ml game stock
- 2 tomatoes on the vine, chopped
- 4 garlic cloves, peeled and crushed, plus 1 extra
- salt and pepper
- 2 sprigs of parsley
- 2 sprigs of thyme
- 1 bay leaf
- 1 duck, jointed in 8 pieces
- 6 good-quality pork sausages, cut in half
- 3 tbsp duck fat
- two 400-g tins haricot beans, drained
- 2 slices of stale sourdough bread, blitzed into crumbs

EQUIPMENT
- ovenproof casserole dish
- baking tray

Alternatives

ready-confit duck joints

Preheat the oven to 220°C/425°F/Gas 7.

Begin with a pan for the stock; you will need a larger ovenproof casserole dish for the whole cassoulet, but start with the stock pan on the hob and heat a large splash of olive oil in it. Add the sliced onions and cook for 10 minutes over a medium heat, until soft. Add the chopped bacon and cook until it is golden and sticky, about 5 minutes.

Pour in the stock, then add the tomatoes, the crushed garlic, some salt and pepper, the parsley, thyme and bay leaf and bring to a slow simmer. Leave to simmer for about 20 minutes. I think this is the tastiest stock I have ever made, by the way. Reserve the stock for later.

Meanwhile, put the duck on a baking tray and place in the oven for 10–15 minutes, then leave to rest. You can omit this step if you decide to use ready-confit duck. Lower the oven temperature to 160°C/325°F/Gas 3.

Cut the remaining garlic clove in half, then use to rub the inside of the large ovenproof casserole that you are going to use for the cassoulet. Add the sausages, along with the duck fat, then add the duck, nestling them all together.

Tip the haricot beans over the top, then pour the stock and all its contents over the top of everything. Bring to the boil on the hob, then sprinkle a few handfuls of breadcrumbs over the top.

Cook the cassoulet in the oven for an hour. The stock will soak into the meat and the beans, and a lovely golden crust will form on top. Delicious... Just serve it as it is.

I've been making this terrine for about ten years now – Adrian brought it into my life. It always makes an appearance at our annual 'Twixmas' party. Serve it with hot toast and pickled damsons, spiced apple chutney, sweet pickled cucumber or just a few little cornichons. It's perfect to keep in the fridge over Christmas, if you can find the time to make it in advance in case you need a snack or guests arrive for lunch. It has a lovely rich flavour, spiced, moist game and creamy chicken livers... delicious.

Game, Pistachio and Juniper Terrine

SERVES 10

- 2 rabbits or 2 wild duck or 4 pigeons or 1 pheasant or a mixture
- salt and pepper
- 800g sausage meat
- 2 tbsp brandy
- 1 garlic clove, peeled and grated
- 5 juniper berries, crushed and chopped
- 1 sprig of thyme
- 250g chicken livers, roughly chopped and gristly bits discarded
- 50g pistachios or blanched almonds or hazelnuts
- butter, for greasing
- 3 bay leaves, preferably fresh
- 600g unsmoked streaky bacon, thinly sliced

EQUIPMENT
- 30-cm terrine tin
- meat thermometer or meat probe
- deep baking tray

Preheat the oven to 200°C/400°F/Gas 6. Whatever your chosen game you will need to part-cook it in the oven first. If using rabbit, duck or pheasant, roast whole on a tray for 20 minutes; for pigeon reduce the time to 15 minutes.

Leave the game until cool enough to handle, then cut off the breasts and legs and shred every scrap of meat into bite-size pieces. This is best done by hand. Season with a little salt and pepper.

While the meat is cooking and cooling, prepare the sausage meat. Add the brandy, garlic, juniper berries, thyme leaves, chicken livers and a large pinch of salt and pepper to a bowl, then the pistachios and mix together. I like the added texture of a nut, and a little pop of bright green when you cut the terrine open.

Preheat the oven to 150°C/300°F/Gas 2. Grease the terrine tin with butter and place the bay leaves on the base. These look pretty when you turn it out, but they also add flavour as the terrine steams in the oven. Line the base and sides with the bacon, leaving longer pieces hanging out so you can wrap them over and also seal the top.

Start to layer up the sausage meat mix and the game into the tin, starting and ending with a layer of sausage meat. You will have three layers of sausage meat and two layers of game meat in between. Add one-third of the sausage meat mix to the bottom of the tin and flatten it down with your hands into a pressed layer. Add half of the game meat and spread it out evenly over the sausage meat. Press it down with your palm, then add the next third of sausage meat, then the remaining game meat, then the final

layer of sausage meat, pressing down the layers in between. Fold over the bacon, sealing up the top. Add a few extra bits of bacon here and there if you have any gaps.

Cover with a piece of greaseproof paper slightly larger than the tin, and tie this on with a piece of string. Place the terrine in a large deep baking tray and fill with warm water until it is about halfway up the side of the terrine tin. Cook in the oven for about an hour, or until the terrine has come away from the edges of the tin. If you want to test it with a meat thermometer or probe, the internal temperature should be about 68°C.

Remove the tray from the oven and take out the terrine. Carefully pour the water out of the tray, then place the terrine back in. Cover with another layer of greaseproof paper, then place some weights or ideally another terrine tin filled with weights, tins, etc. on top. I have been known to use 11/2 bricks, which fit nicely. Leave to stand overnight. I find it's best to then leave it in its tin for a further day in the fridge for the flavours to really develop.

When ready to eat, loosen the edge of the terrine with a knife and then turn it upside down onto a board to remove the terrine from the tin, discarding any fat and jelly surrounding it, then slice and eat.

NOTES

This recipe is changeable depending on the season and what is to hand. For a duck terrine I use two small wild ducks, for pigeon you need four birds or you can use a whole poached chicken.

Alternatives

pheasant; pigeon; duck

Advice

Keep the carcasses to make stock if you wish – it's lovely for a cassoulet.

Buy your sausagemeat from the butcher. You want it to have a decent amount of fat in it; minced meat in the supermarkets these days is fatless to the point of ridiculousness.

A chef around the corner from me had a deer going spare: 'head off, hoofs off, skin on,' did I want it? Of course I did. My butcher showed me what to do with the carcass and I have to say, using this recipe, it was the most delicious venison I have ever had. The meat is on the rare side of medium rare, and is so beautifully soft with a seared crust seasoned with lots of herbs and butter. I can't tell you how much I have enjoyed both of the loins, each as delicious as the other, served with sticky beetroot and red cabbage and some celeriac mash with lots of butter and a bit of nutmeg.

Venison Loin Pan-fried in Butter and Thyme

SERVES 4 or 2 gluttons

- 1 venison loin
- salt and pepper
- olive oil, for the pan
- 20g butter
- 1 garlic clove, peeled and crushed
- 1 sprig of thyme

Alternatives
fillet of beef

Bring the loin to room temperature, for at least an hour, maybe more, then dry it thoroughly with kitchen roll and season generously with salt and pepper. You will need more seasoning than you think – as if you were salting a pavement, I read somewhere...

Add a tiny bit of oil to a large heavy-based frying pan, which should be big enough to hold the loin in one piece and wipe the oil over the pan with kitchen roll. Place the pan over a very high heat and, when hot, add the venison; it should sizzle loudly as it hits the pan, turn the heat down slightly. Do not move the meat or touch or press it, just leave to cook for 2 minutes. The pan should be hot, but if it smells like it's burning then turn it down a touch. After 2 minutes turn the loin onto the other side and cook for 2 more minutes. It should have taken on a lovely golden colour. Again, don't touch it or move it, just leave it.

When the loin has had 2 minutes on each side, turn the heat off and add the butter, along with the crushed garlic and thyme. Baste the meat for 10 minutes, spooning over the delicious melted butter that has picked up all the flavours of the meat, garlic and thyme. The pan will have retained enough heat to keep it warm while finishing off in the butter.

Finally, remove the loin and leave to rest somewhere warm for 5 minutes. Carve the meat into 2-cm slices, drizzle the pan juices over the meat and serve.

This recipe is a type of *daube* with venison. A *daube* is a classic French stew made with beef, which is slow-cooked with wine and vegetables and is often flavoured with duck fat, vinegar, brandy, lavender, nutmeg, cinnamon, cloves, juniper berries or orange peel. They used to be left cooking on the hearth for the whole day, and are often better made the day before. This is my venison version.

When it is done the carrots taste so much of orange, with a rich red wine gravy tasting of delicate herbs, and the venison is soft and falling apart with smoky bacon and soft onions. I serve it with creamy mashed potato or buttery polenta.

Venison and Wild Mushroom Ragu

Put the wild mushrooms into a heatproof bowl and cover with the boiling water. Leave to stand until you are ready for them.

Place the flour on a plate and season with a pinch of salt and pepper. Toss the meat in the seasoned flour. Heat the olive oil in a frying pan over a medium heat and when hot start adding batches of the meat to brown. You may have to do this in a few batches. If you add too much, the meat will start to stew in its juices rather than browning nicely. When the meat is browned all over, put it into a large casserole dish.

Add the bacon lardons to the same pan, and fry these off until golden, then add them to the venison in the casserole dish. Fry the onion in the same pan again, adding a little more oil if necessary, until soft and golden, about 5 minutes. Transfer them to the casserole.

Keep the frying pan over a high heat and add about a glass of red wine to deglaze it. You want to scrape up all of the flavour and bits that have stuck to the pan and mix them into the wine as it bubbles away furiously. Pour this into the casserole after a few minutes. Put the casserole dish over a low heat and mix the venison, bacon, onion and wine together, then add the rest of the wine. Pour in the mushrooms and the soaking water too.

Add the carrot, thyme, bay leaf, juniper berries, garlic and orange peel, then leave to simmer very gently, with the lid on, for 2 hours. Keep it over a low heat and stir occasionally. When it is ready, the meat should be soft and falling apart.

SERVES 2-3

- 50g mixed dried wild mushrooms
- 100ml boiling water
- 50g plain flour
- salt and pepper
- 500g venison stewing meat, in bite-size pieces
- 1 tbsp olive oil
- 100g smoked bacon lardons
- 1 medium onion, peeled and sliced into thin rounds
- 1/2 bottle of red wine you like
- 1 carrot, peeled and sliced
- 1 sprig of thyme
- 1 bay leaf
- 4 juniper berries, crushed
- 1 garlic clove, peeled and sliced
- 1 large piece of orange peel

EQUIPMENT
- large ovenproof casserole dish

I cook this much less than I used to, but for years it was a go-to midweek dinner. Lentils get a bad rep, but when cooked slowly with bacon, wine and stock I love them. Topped with delicious fat sausages and this almost buttery, mustard apple sauce, they are a delicious dinner on a cold winter's evening.

You can make the apple mustard in advance. It's a Danish recipe in origin and goes well with these sausages and lentils but also with roast pork, barbecued pork ribs, cheese or sausage rolls! It keeps well in the fridge for a month.

Sausage and Lentils with Apple Mustard

SERVES 4

LENTILS AND SAUSAGES
- 2 splashes of olive oil
- 1 onion, peeled and diced into small cubes
- 1 carrot, peeled and diced into small cubes
- 1 celery stick, trimmed and diced into small cubes
- 100g pancetta, diced
- 1 bay leaf
- 2 garlic cloves, peeled and crushed
- 1 sprig of thyme
- 250g Puy lentils
- 100ml white wine
- 1 litre chicken stock
- salt and pepper
- 8 fat good-quality sausages

EQUIPMENT
- baking tray

For the lentils, heat a splash of olive oil in a large pan over a medium heat. Tip the onion, carrot and celery into the pan and cook until they have softened and taken on a little golden colour, about 15 minutes. Add the pancetta and cook until it has taken on a little colour, another 5 minutes. Add the bay leaf, garlic and thyme, then add the lentils.

Pour in the wine and bring to the boil. Boil for 2 minutes, letting the alcohol burn off. You should be able to smell when it has gone. Add the stock to cover and simmer for about 40 minutes. Do not season until the end as adding salt beforehand can prevent the lentils softening.

Meanwhile, preheat the oven to 190°C/375°F/Gas 5. Arrange the sausages on a baking tray with a little splash of olive oil, then roast in the oven for 20 minutes, or until golden brown.

To serve, spoon the lentils into a bowl and top with sausages and a dollop of the apple mustard.

To make the apple mustard, put the apples into a large pan with the water, cover with a lid and steam for 8 minutes, or until they start to break down a little but some pieces remain.

Pour the apples into a blender and blend well for a few minutes, then strain everything through a sieve into a bowl, to catch any pips or core remaining. Stir in the vinegar, sugar, mustard and salt. You can pot it up into sterilized jars (see page 280) and keep it in the fridge for months – it will make about 3 x 225g jars.

SERVES 4

APPLE MUSTARD

- 6 Braeburn apples or similar, roughly chopped, skin and core left on
- 3 tbsp water
- 4 tbsp white wine vinegar
- 2 tbsp light muscovado sugar
- 2 tbsp Dijon mustard
- pinch of salt

EQUIPMENT

- blender

I served this at my very first supper club. It takes a long time, but when it's ready it just falls apart and is so juicy and unctuous. The skin is blackened and crispy but still delicious and the meat couldn't be softer. A pile of soft, sweet pork falling apart with some crispy polenta chips, creamy, crunchy coleslaw, sweet, smoky baked beans, and a bit of tangy barbecue sauce on the side; what could be better in life?

Slow-roast Pork Shoulder with Paprika, Mustard and Baked Beans

SERVES 8-10

PORK
- 2kg pork shoulder, boned, rolled and tied by your butcher
- 2 tbsp English mustard
- 1 tbsp caster sugar
- 1 tbsp smoked paprika
- 1 tsp salt
- 1 tsp ground black pepper
- 500ml water

BAKED BEANS
- 100g pancetta, chopped
- 1 onion, peeled and chopped
- 1 garlic clove, peeled and grated
- 250ml water
- 60ml ketchup
- 2 tbsp maple syrup
- 2 tbsp sunflower oil
- 1 tbsp white wine vinegar
- 2 tbsp English mustard
- 1/2 tsp ground black pepper
- 1 bay leaf
- good pinch of salt
- two 400-g tins haricot beans, drained

Preheat the oven to 130°C/250°F/Gas 1. Take the pork shoulder and heavily smear it in the mustard, sugar, paprika, salt and pepper. Pour 500ml water into the bottom of the tin, add the pork and cook in the oven for 9 whole hours.

I like recipes that you can describe in one or two sentences. After 5 hours, cover the pork with foil and make sure it always has some liquid in the bottom of the tray. Your house will smell amazing.

The baked beans were inspired by a recipe for some lentils in *The Art of Living According to Joe Beef* which I adapted to suit. Fry the pancetta and onion until golden and soft, then add the garlic. Next, add the water, ketchup, maple syrup, sunflower oil, vinegar, mustard, black pepper, bay leaf, some salt and finally the haricot beans. Cover with a lid and simmer for 30 minutes, checking it and stirring occasionally, adding a bit more water if need be. Shred the pork before serving.

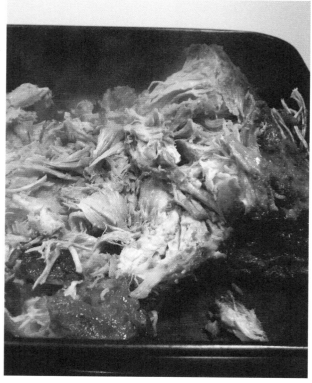

This recipe has a lot of different versions in my kitchen, but I have found this one to be my most recent favourite. The pickled walnuts and a splash of their liquid makes the stew so interesting and delicious, then topped with fresh dill it combines a lot of my best-loved flavours. The beef just falls apart and melts into the sauce. It is great served with buttery new potatoes or mash, or throw in some butter beans and kale at the end. You can also use ox cheek instead of shin and tail, or as well as, if you like.

Beer-braised Oxtail and Shin Stew with Pickled Walnuts and Dill

Preheat the oven to 180°C/350°F/Gas 4. Heat the oil and butter in a heavy-based pan, add the onions and cook for 10 minutes over a medium heat, or until soft and golden.

Place the meat in the large oven tray and season it generously with salt and pepper. Add the pear, skin, stalk and core included. Add the carrots, garlic and thyme, then add the cooked onions and mix everything together.

Add the capers, pickled walnuts and pickling liquid, then pour in the dark beer and chicken stock to almost cover everything. Top up with water if needs be. Be careful not to fill the tray too full of liquid as you need to move it in and out of the oven.

Cover the tray tightly with foil and put it in the oven for 3 hours. Check it halfway through, turning the meat and making sure it still full of liquid.

Serve topped with dill and new potatoes covered in butter.

NOTES
Don't throw the pear stalk, skin or core away as it is all added to the meat.

SERVES 6-8

- 1 tbsp olive oil
- 20g butter
- 2 onions, peeled and sliced
- 800g beef shin, diced
- 1kg oxtail, cut into rounds by the butcher
- salt and pepper
- 1 pear, halved, peeled, cored and roughly chopped (see Notes)
- 2 carrots, peeled and roughly chopped
- 3 garlic cloves, peeled and crushed
- 1 sprig of thyme or savory
- 1 handful of capers
- 5 pickled walnuts, chopped
- 6 tbsp walnut pickling liquid
- 300ml dark beer
- 500ml chicken stock
- chopped dill, for topping

EQUIPMENT
- large oven tray, about 6cm deep

On a jaunt to London, we found ourselves hungry in Brick Lane, mid-afternoon, near the famous Brick Lane bagel shop, so we queued and ordered salt beef bagels, and my God they were good... If you have never made your own bagels and like baking you must try it. It's hugely satisfying, and homemade bagels are just a whole different species from shop-bought ones–the recipe is on page 270.

Salt Beef, Bagels and Sweet Cucumber Pickle

SERVES 10

CURING
- 200g caster sugar
- 300g sea salt
- 6 juniper berries
- 4 cloves
- 6 black peppercorns
- 2 bay leaves
- 2 litres water
- 15g Prague powder #1 or cure #1 (see Notes)
- 2kg brisket

COOKING
- 1 onion, cut in half
- 1 carrot, cut in half
- 2 bay leaves
- 1 sprig of parsley
- 1 celery stick
- 6 black peppercorns
- 3 juniper berries, crushed

EQUIPMENT
- large Tupperware bucket

To cure the beef, in a large pan, combine the sugar, sea salt, juniper berries, cloves, peppercorns, bay leaves, water and Prague powder #1 or cure #1. Stir well and bring to the boil to dissolve the salt and sugar, then leave to cool to room temperature.

I usually brine a whole brisket at a time in a large Tupperware container that I keep at the bottom of the fridge. Cut the meat up into large pieces to fit your container – a deep Tupperware is ideal; then pour over the brine and weigh it down with a few plates to keep the meat fully submerged under the liquid. Cover with a lid and put it in the fridge. If you are only doing a small quantity you can put it in a freezer bag and fill that with the brine and just turn it over each day. I have left it to brine for anything from 5–15 days, but a week is ideal. Turn the meat around every couple of days, so it cures evenly.

When you are ready to cook the beef, remove it from the brine, place it in a large pan with the onion, carrot, bay leaves, parsley, celery, peppercorns, juniper berries and lots of cold water so it is fully covered. Bring to the boil, reduce the heat and simmer very gently for 4 hours.

After 4 hours the meat will fall apart into lovely pink shreds. You can serve it hot with horseradish cream and potatoes, or pull it apart and put it in a bagel with lots of Sweet Cucumber Pickle (see page 295)and English mustard. It's a delight.

NOTES
I add Prague powder #1 or cure #1 to the brine. It contains saltpetre, a curing agent, which encourages the meat to turn that lovely pink colour and cure evenly. You can buy this online.

These amounts make 2 litres of brine, which is enough to brine 2kg brisket. You can also use this brine for lots of other recipes too, including pork belly and ox tongue.

I like this served in summer with delicious sauces, a fresh cucumber and herb salad and flatbreads to mop it up, or I turn it into my own little kebabs. It is so good with the Sweet Cumin Yoghurt and the Smoky Aubergine Yoghurt (see page 51). Just throw in a spicy tomato sauce and serve with a big bowl of buttery couscous on the side and you have one of my favourite meals of all time. For best flavour, marinate the lamb in the spices overnight.

Slow-roast Spiced Lamb Shoulder

In a small pan, combine the peppercorns, cardamom, fennel, cumin and coriander seeds, star anise and cinnamon and toast over a high heat for 1–2 minutes until you can smell the spices. Add the nutmeg and paprika and toast for a few seconds more, then transfer all the spices to a pestle and mortar and grind to a fine powder. Use a spice grinder if you have one.

Put the spice mix into a large bowl, add the salt, ginger, garlic, lemon juice and olive oil and mix it all together.

Jab the lamb shoulder all over with a small knife so the flavours of the marinade can get right in. Place the lamb in a large roasting tin and rub the marinade all over, into every crevice. Cover with foil or clingfilm, then leave to marinate for a few hours, or overnight in the fridge if possible.

If the meat has been in the fridge overnight ,then bring it out to warm up a couple of hours before you want to cook it, still in the tin. Preheat the oven to 150°C/300°F/Gas 2. Add the shallots and garlic to the tin, then pour in the white wine and chicken stock. Cover tightly with foil and roast for 4 hours, checking a couple of times and making sure the liquid is topped up in the bottom of the tray.

To finish, increase the oven temperature to 220°C/425°F/Gas 7, then uncover the lamb and blast it for 15 minutes to crisp up the skin.

SERVES 4

- 1 tsp black peppercorns
- 1/2 tsp cardamom seeds
- 1 tsp fennel seeds
- 1 tbsp cumin seeds
- 1 tsp coriander seeds
- 1 star anise
- 1/2 cinnamon stick
- 1 tsp grated nutmeg
- 1 tbsp sweet smoked paprika
- 1 tbsp salt
- 20g piece of fresh ginger, peeled and grated
- 3 garlic cloves, peeled and grated
- 30ml lemon juice
- 50ml olive oil
- 1/2 lamb shoulder, 1kg
- 3 banana shallots, peeled and roughly chopped
- 4 garlic cloves, peeled and roughly chopped
- 250ml white wine
- 250ml chicken stock

EQUIPMENT
- pestle and mortar
- large roasting tin

NOTES

I prefer the blade end of the shoulder, as it is fattier; the other end is the knuckle. If you have more than four people to feed, just get a whole shoulder.

These meatballs were just a bit off the cuff on a Friday night faffing about in the kitchen. I had a packet of goat mince and made it up as I went along. They turned out to be an absolute triumph, and one that I have continued to make frequently. I flavour the meatballs with fennel and coriander seeds, roast them and toss them in a roast tomato and red pepper sauce; it's so delicious! If you haven't had much goat in the past I would highly recommend it – it's not as strong as lamb or beef, just a really delicate, beautiful flavour.

Goat Mince Meatballs with Roast Tomato Sauce and Polenta

SERVES 2-3

- 200g tomatoes on the vine
- olive oil, for cooking
- salt and pepper
- 1 tsp caster sugar
- 1 slice of slightly stale sourdough bread, crusts removed
- 2 tbsp milk
- 1 tsp coriander seeds
- 1/2 tsp fennel seeds
- 400g minced goat meat
- 1/2 onion, peeled and finely chopped, plus 1 onion, peeled and sliced
- 1 garlic clove, peeled and grated
- 1 red pepper, thinly sliced
- butter, for cooking
- chopped sage, for topping

EQUIPMENT
- baking tray
- blender or food processor
- pestle and mortar

Alternatives
lamb

Preheat the oven to 200°C/400°F/Gas 6.

Cut the tomatoes into quarters and pop them into a baking tray. Add a generous splash of olive oil, a pinch of salt, the sugar and some black pepper, mix well and then pop them in the oven for 30 minutes, or until they start to look a bit sticky and caramelized. Keep an eye on them as all tomatoes differ. You want it to start to colour and most of the water to cook away.

When the tomatoes are done, tip them into a small blender and blitz until smooth. They should almost become creamy. (It's my new favourite way of making a tomato sauce, especially while tomatoes are in season; I much prefer this roasted fresh tomato method over using tins.)

While you are waiting for the tomatoes, start the meatballs. Blitz the bread into fine crumbs in a small blender or food processor. Put the breadcrumbs into a bowl, add the milk and leave them to soak.

Toast the coriander and fennel seeds in a small dry frying pan until you can smell them, just a few minutes, then pop them into a pestle and mortar and grind to a rough powder. Crumble the minced meat into a large bowl and add the spices. Add the chopped onion, garlic, a big pinch of salt, some pepper and the breadcrumbs and mix together to combine. Divide the mixture into balls about 20g each, and roll together in your hands, about the size of a golf ball.

Put the meatballs into a baking tray with some olive oil and the red pepper, coating everything in oil before putting them in the oven. Bake them for 25 minutes, but give them a shake after 10 minutes. They should take on a bit of colour but you don't want them to cook for too long and dry out.

Meanwhile, heat a little oil and butter in a frying pan over a medium heat, add the sliced onion and cook until golden, about 10 minutes, then added the blitzed tomato sauce to the pan to warm through. A lot of fat can come out of the meatballs, which is great as they end up so juicy, but instead of adding the sauce to the baking tray scoop them out of the fat with the peppers and toss them into the tomato sauce in the pan.

Top with some chopped sage and serve with some buttery polenta.

NOTES

I used 400g of goat meat for two people; this is quite generous, and would feed three easily! I get my goat meat from The Goat Company, who trade locally. Buy a few packs when you see it and keep it in the freezer – it really is such delicious meat.

There's a guy in Newcastle who smokes stuff; he has a stall at my monthly food market and each month turns up with something new he has tried out – nuts, cheese, chillies, black pudding, chicken, eggs (not convinced) are staples. One month he turned up with some whiskey oak smoked brown sugar. I somehow resisted the temptation to not just spoon it straight into my mouth, the smell and taste are just so good...

These ribs are covered in a sticky smoky marinade and then slow cooked until they just fall apart. Even if you can't find smoked sugar you will still be rewarded.

Slow-roast Beef Short Ribs with Treacle, Thyme and Smoked Sugar

Preheat the oven to 160°C/325°F/Gas 3.

Combine the sugar or paprika, if using, the treacle, coriander seeds, chilli flakes and mustard into a thick paste and rub it all over the ribs with your hands, getting it into all of the crevices, then sprinkle with salt and pepper well.

Lay the ribs in a deep baking tray, with enough room for them to fit, but not too much spare space. Throw in the garlic cloves, thyme and rosemary. Pour in the beer – any will do, use one you like – then top up with the beef bone stock until the liquid almost covers the ribs. Cover tightly with foil and cook in the oven for 3 hours, turning the ribs halfway through.

After 3 hours remove the foil and increase the oven temperature to 200°C/400°F/Gas 6 and cook for another 10 minutes. This will give them a burst of heat and get the fat to crisp up a bit while staying beautifully soft on the inside. The ribs will just fall apart.

Spoon some of the sweet sticky juices over the ribs and serve with buttery polenta or mash and a dollop of English mustard.

SERVES 6

- 35g smoked brown sugar or 35g soft brown sugar and 1 tsp smoked paprika
- 2 tbsp dark treacle
- 2 tsp crushed coriander seeds
- 1 tsp chilli flakes
- 2 tbsp English mustard
- 6 beef short ribs
- salt and pepper
- 6 garlic cloves, peeled but left whole
- 1 sprig of thyme
- 1 sprig of rosemary
- 1 bottle beer, of your choice
- 1 litre beef stock

Alternatives
ox cheek; oxtail; beef shin

How To...

Cook a Lamb in the Ground

In short these instructions are as follows: dig a hole in the ground, fill it with stones, light a fire until the stones are red hot, put in the lamb tightly wrapped in foil and cloth, cover with soil and turf and hope for the best... Really, I can tell you what to do approximately, but the best way is just to have a go and then you'll know!

01 **What you need:** Somewhere you can dig a pit, a spade, large stones or bricks, kindling and logs, a leg of lamb, a marinade mix, fireproof gloves, a damp old towel and foil.

02 **The pit:** This needs to be deep enough to accommodate two layers of stones with the lamb in the middle – about half a metre deep, and the same in width and length. Keep the soil and the turf lid as you will put these back over the top once the lamb is in.

03 **Starting the fire:** Line the bottom and the edges of the pit with the stones. Cover with kindling and logs and get the fire going, gradually adding more logs.

04 **The lamb:** Marinate the leg of lamb in whatever you fancy. I chose garlic, rosemary, lovage, olive oil, lemon juice, salt and pepper and left it out to come up to room temperature. Before it goes in it needs to be wrapped very tightly in layers of foil, but do this carefully so the juices

don't leak out. Finally, wrap it in an old damp towel to create a barrier between the lamb and stones and prevent burnt spots.

05 **The cooking:** Slowly let the fire burn right down, pushing the embers away into the gaps between the stones, until it has all but disappeared and you are left with red-hot stones.

06 **Putting the lamb on to cook:** Use fireproof gloves to lift out some of the stones, put the lamb in the

middle, then put some stones back over the top, and around the edges so all surfaces are covered. Dig the soil back over, so no jets of steam are escaping, and put the turf back on top, stamping it down. You shouldn't be able to feel any heat coming out at all. Cook for 10 hours, either starting early in the morning to serve at dinner, or overnight for lunch.

07 **Serving:** Carefully lift the turf lid, then begin to dig away the soil, slowly uncovering the bundle – once unwrapped the lamb should be beautifully cooked!

Building a Tiny Restaurant in the Middle of Nowhere

The shipping containers were already like home to me. I knew which of the ten different keys went in the ten different padlocks and I knew which lever to pull in which order to release the huge metal doors. They slowly creaked open and there it was: my new home.

The space is two shipping containers side by side, one thirty feet and one forty feet long. They are tucked back from the street a little, surrounded by trees, and the sun dances through the leaves from morning through to afternoon. Something about the proportions of the space and the ever-changing light have always made it feel like a comfortable place to be. I had a good feeling standing there, with my own set of keys and my own plans ahead, but I was essentially looking at an empty box.

The two containers are side by side and slightly offset, with the overlapping middle walls cut out to create a larger area as you enter. The two ends – the entrance and the doors to the back garden – are both fully glazed. There are small slot-like windows cut into the sides for extra light, and the external areas created front and back by offsetting the containers create two gardens of sorts.

At this point the plywood walls and floors were unfinished and unpainted and the back garden was a pile of rubble; there was a sink in one corner and there was a toilet, but that was essentially it. There was a lot of work to do and it was time to get on with it. I had saved as much money as I could through running supper clubs and larger events with the National Trust. It was just enough to get going – £8000 if I remember rightly – a drop in the ocean compared to the average restaurant start-up budget.

My head was full of questions. How do you set up a company? How does service work? What will environmental health say? Who will come? Should I make my own butter? Does it matter if there's no gas? What should it be called? Can I actually do this? Where should I get bread from? What should be on the menu? Who grows veg round here? How long can I afford not to have an income? Is it OK if I only serve pour-over coffee? Does anyone even walk down this street? How will people know I'm here? How do I get a business bank account? How much does a website cost? Can I manage this on my own? What's the long-term plan? Am I mad?

Some of the questions were easy to answer and some played on my mind for months. Each had a solution, however, which I figured out along the way. People were friendly and helpful, as the food community in Newcastle is an encouraging place with people always eager to help. When I was too embarrassed to ask the really stupid questions, there was always Google.

To add to the pressure, in between leaving my job and opening up I decided to go and work in a couple of London restaurants for a few weeks to expand my knowledge and skills. I wanted to check if I knew what I was doing. I could have done that at home but I wanted to challenge myself. A good friend was managing Quo Vadis in Soho at the time and put me in touch with chef Jeremy Lee, who was happy for me to go and 'stage', as it is known, in their kitchen. Another introduction to one of my long-term heroes, Margot Henderson, saw me nervously pressing the buzzer at Rochelle Canteen a few weeks later.

I arrived to some confusion, but once everyone realized why I was there, I was kitted out as a chef for the first time and set to work. Washing nettles was the first task – a good one to begin with as I could settle down and survey my surroundings. I was pretty happy standing there washing the nettles and smiling to myself that I was actually doing this.

Standing in the Rochelle Canteen kitchen surrounded by their team of chefs, it was easy to feel that I knew very little at all. I was there to learn, though: how they organized themselves (very well), how long they kept things, when they ordered stuff, how they reused leftovers, recipes, ideas, presentation; I wanted to know everything. So I set to it... Cut, chop, prep, observe, clean, watch and learn. Anna Tobias was the head chef at Rochelle

Canteen, running a tight little ship, confidently and efficiently sending out tasty, interesting dishes everyday as well as catering for events. My first day's work over, we all sat down for the staff lunch, which included leftover rabbit faggots with mash, salad and lemony roast chicken, followed by some leftover blood orange sorbet and golden syrup biscotti. Well, you don't get much better than that in my books. I was (nervously) having a wonderful time.

The following week I was so terrified about working at Quo Vadis that I started to grind my teeth in my sleep, waking up in agony. However, it turned out that Jeremy Lee greeted everyone with kisses and had such a lovely group of friendly and encouraging chefs in his kitchen that I felt better as soon as I arrived.

It was a much bigger set-up than Rochelle Canteen. I spent time in different sections with different chefs, even a couple who had studied architecture – one in Newcastle. I spent some time in bread and pastry, butchery, fish and sauces, as well as plating up and sending out some of the starters, which I loved. I left London exhausted but full of knowledge and ideas.

Back in Newcastle I began by painting: walls, floors and window frames in subtly different shades of white, blue and grey. I bought nice but cheap garden furniture from a camping website and painted that too. I had a

palette in my head of pale duck egg blues, bleached-out woods, pale green succulents in pots, enamel plates, natural linen fabrics, botanical prints; I could see it all in my mind, I just needed to make it real. One of the things I loved about working in the design world was this stage, gathering a beautiful palette of ideas. But this time I was the client, and I hoped I wouldn't hate the project by the end!

I gathered cooking equipment as cheaply as I could. The oven was the main expense and even then it was just a domestic double oven with an in-built induction hob. There was no gas on the site so I toyed with the idea of installing Calor gas bottles outside and piping it in, but that soon became very complicated so I settled for everything being electric.

I bought a small pot-belly wood-burning stove on eBay, which was made out of a converted Calor gas bottle. It's extremely cosy in winter, and definitely needed – winter in a shipping container can be challenging at points, particularly when the toilet freezes… I cleared the rubble from the garden and got someone in to lay some decking, which was expensive – hence why it doesn't extend very far! – and I filled some massive grow bags from eBay with herbs and courgettes, hoping for a bit of produce for when I opened. I got the builders in for everything I couldn't do: building new walls for the toilet and the store, hardwiring the oven, installing the kitchen extractor fan… I costed out every penny, made spreadsheets for everything and watched my bank account slowly drain away.

I organized my bin collection, applied to run a food business with the council, set up a bank account and a limited company. I researched a lot and spoke to a lot of people: people in hospitality, chef friends, my butcher, other people I knew with small businesses, friends in food, people with successful food businesses… There was no shortage of helpful advice and I slowly pieced it all together until I had formed my own views. I'm still proud I managed to sort it all out myself, more or less. I just made lots of lists and got on with it.

I had a few well-paid supper clubs booked in over this time, which was a saving grace. One involved a trip to London, where the brief was 'Northumberland'. I had to travel with a 'mobile' fridge on wheels full of local produce on the train, as I couldn't afford to hire a refrigerated van. Turned out these things weren't very mobile. I was travelling with 10kg of local lamb and a crate of North Sea lobsters, and it was really heavy and really hard work! I could have done without that, but it was a boost to the bank account and allowed me to carry on.

    I printed out our new menus, put lights up, tested food, framed pictures and gradually it was becoming the place I had imagined. I got Environmental Health round to advise me, which wasn't as scary as I had imagined. They were incredibly helpful, and didn't even think it was a ridiculous idea to open a restaurant in a shipping container.

I even designed my own branding. The idea for this came from the rail in my kitchen at home where I hang my cooking utensils: I had a bunch of bay leaves drying out on it and used some artistic licence and added a leg of ham. I was really pleased with it and still proudly say, 'I did!' when people ask who designed it. Once printed and put up as signage, with our name, Cook House, everything suddenly began to feel very real.

It was actually starting to look like a real restaurant/kitchen/café. I still wasn't sure how to explain it to people. People asked constantly when I was opening. It changed all the time as things took longer to finish or arrange than I thought, so I just took to saying, 'Soon…'

FIRE

Fire

Wherever possible I make plans to light fires: by the river, in the wild, even right outside my house in my one-metre strip of garden – no space is too small. I'm not sure how the neighbours feel about it sometimes, when the smoke is billowing down the street! Sometimes these fire plans are quite extravagant – such as cooking a whole venison and river trout at the top of a deserted valley with friends and family one summer. I'll send out invitations with just a little map; everyone will walk for miles to the delight at the end.

It feels like such an achievement, starting a fire and then keeping it going. Huddled on a little beach in Scotland in the winter, we built a fire and cooked some scallops over it. This was so much more enjoyable than if we had just stood in front of the rental kitchen oven. It's communal, it's exciting and it's lovely to watch.

Give the vegetables a chance, too, when it comes to fire: on the grill or wrapped up and cooked in the embers, charred to within a centimetre of their life and folded through yoghurt, they have a lot to bring to the table!

For all of these recipes you should light your barbecue or fire about 45 minutes before you want to start cooking. It is better to have too much charcoal on the barbecue than too little – running out of heat as you throw the steak on is enough to make you cry. I use lumpwood charcoal as the larger pieces burn longer than the smaller bits. Those briquette things should be avoided at all costs. Also invest in a blowtorch, as it makes lighting the barbecue fast and argument-free.

The key to successful barbecuing is to have everything ready in advance. Do everything ahead of time: salads, sauces, sides; set the table, warm lots of bowls and plates, pour drinks and get everything on the table so as soon as the food comes off the grill you can all dig in!

Your coals should be white, grey and red-hot, and the flames should have died down before you start cooking. Shut down any vents at this stage and the fire will retain its heat and not burn out too quickly. It will be hottest in the middle, less towards the edges. Work out your order of cooking before you begin, thinking about what might need to rest, what goes cold quickly and what takes the longest and least time to cook, then form a plan. This is when you realize not cooking too many different things is a good idea. Ingredients such as vegetables and sausages can be cooked in the middle to get some char and colour, then can be moved to the edge to continue cooking more slowly while you use the hottest spot for something else, such as a big steak or whole fish.

Traditionally this has always been my favourite barbecued meal – lamb shish kebabs with salads, sauces and toasted pittas. A trio of the best sauces is what makes it for me – spicy thick tomato sauce, a Smoky Aubergine Yoghurt (see page 51) and a Sweet Cumin Yoghurt (see page 51). They all complement each other perfectly alongside the lamb and a simple chopped salad.

BBQ Lamb Shoulder Kebabs with Spicy Tomato Sauce

SERVES 4

- 1 small cucumber, diced
- 1 handful of cherry tomatoes, diced
- 1/4 red onion, peeled and finely diced
- 1 handful each of parsley and mint, chopped
- olive oil, to season
- salt and pepper

LAMB KEBABS

- 550g diced lamb shoulder
- olive oil, for cooking
- 1 sprig of rosemary, chopped

TOMATO SAUCE

- 1/2 onion, peeled and chopped
- 1 garlic clove, peeled and grated
- pinch of chilli flakes
- 400-g tin chopped tomatoes
- 1 tsp caster sugar

EQUIPMENT

- barbecue
- bamboo skewers
- meat thermometer

Light your barbecue or fire about 45 minutes before you want to start cooking Prepare the chopped salad in advance: small cubes of cucumber, tomato and red onion with a large handful of chopped flat leaf parsley and mint and seasoned with olive oil, salt and pepper. Set aside.

Put the cubes of lamb into a large bowl, add a splash of olive oil, salt and pepper and the rosemary, cover and leave to marinate at room temperature until you are ready to grill. Soak several bamboo skewers in a bowl of water to prevent them burning during cooking.

To make the tomato sauce, sweat the onion in oil over a low heat until soft, about 10 minutes, then add the garlic, chilli flakes and tomatoes. Season with salt and pepper and add the sugar. Simmer over a low heat for about 30 minutes, or until the sauce is thick, sweet and spicy.

Finally, thread the lamb onto the soaked wooden skewers, about five pieces of lamb per skewer. Grill on the barbecue for about 3 minutes on each side, or until they are browned all over and still a bit pink in the middle. They should be 50°C in the centre on a meat thermometer. Add a big pile of pitta breads to the barbecue while everyone is helping themselves to kebabs, sauces and salad.

This is less a recipe, more my favourite day ever: friends, a big fire, the great outdoors, some tasty unfussy food, wine and hopefully a bit of sunshine. The lamb is delicious but it's the process that's the best bit – it takes a while so buy lots of crisps and nibbles...The lamb is most flavoursome if marinated overnight, so get started the day before cooking for best results.

Hanging Leg of Lamb by a Tall Fire

SERVES 8

- 1 leg of lamb
- various vegetables, such as beetroot, celeriac, carrots and fennel, wrapped in foil

MARINADE

- 2 tbsp olive oil
- zest of 1 lemon
- 2 garlic cloves, peeled and grated
- 2 sprigs of rosemary
- 2 sprigs of thyme
- salt and pepper

EQUIPMENT

- strong string
- hooks
- something to hang the lamb from a tree
- barbecue tripod if you have one or a self-made tripod made from three long sticks bound together at the top
- a large bag of birch logs
- kindling
- firelighters or newspaper
- meat thermometer

Cover the lamb in the marinade the day before you want to cook it to really get the flavour into it, rubbing it into all the nooks and crannies and leaving it in the fridge overnight. A good few hours before you want to cook the lamb, bring it out of the fridge to warm up.

Then you can build the fire. Make a big circle of stones that will contain the fire; you don't want it to spread. Fill the circle with more stones as a base, which will heat up and radiate out heat, helping to cook the lamb. The idea is to build the fire up and hang the lamb slightly to one side of it so you can spin it and it can cook evenly rather than thrusting it right into the flames.

I bought a barbecue tripod for this purpose, but the first time we rigged our own up with three long lengths of wood arranged like a tepee and bound with string at the top. Tie up the lamb like a parcel with string so no bits of meat are hanging out to burn, then tie a piece of string around the top of the leg to attach a hook to.

Start your fire: you want it to burn high so the flames come up the side of the whole leg of lamb, so keep adding wood in a tepee style. Set up your tripod and suspend the lamb on a piece of strong string suspended from the top, so it hangs just a little way off the ground, and very near the fire, but slightly to one side. You can put a pot under it to catch the juices. I have added beans and tomatoes, too, in the past.

As the fire burns spin the lamb repeatedly in one direction like you are winding it up, then let it go to unwind on its own, so all sides are getting the benefit of the fire. Repeat this over and over. There's probably a machine to do this, but it is quite therapeutic if you take it in turns.

How long it takes to cook will depend on your fire, the weather and the size of lamb, but usually around 1–2 hours. The outside should be crispy and the inside pink, reading 50°C right in the middle on a meat thermometer. You can also wrap up various vegetables in foil and place them in the edges of the fire, turning them occasionally. Beetroot and celeriac work particularly well as they turn out beautifully soft and smoky.

When the lamb is done, leave to rest for 20 minutes, then carve and serve with the fire-roasted vegetables, some garlicky yoghurt, salad and some smoky tomato beans.

I fed five hundred people with this recipe, which is an awful lot of beef! But the beauty of it on the barbecue is that you just put one big piece of meat on the grill, and minutes later you can feed a large crowd. It will get you used to cooking big bits of meat on a grill too, which is exciting and a good skill to have if you enjoy cooking with fire.

BBQ Bavette with Soy, Ginger and Garlic

SERVES 10

- 1 tsp salt
- 1 tsp pepper
- 1 tbsp caster sugar
- 1 tbsp light soy sauce
- 1 garlic clove, peeled and grated
- 2-cm piece of fresh ginger, peeled and grated
- 2kg bavette or skirt steak

EQUIPMENT

- barbecue
- meat thermometer or probe

Combine the salt, pepper, sugar, soy, garlic and ginger in a large bowl. Add the steak, rubbing the marinade into all the nooks and crannies of the meat. Leave to marinate for an hour or two at room temperature. Alternatively, cover and put it in the fridge to marinate overnight. Just make sure you remove it from the fridge 1–2 hours before you are going to cook so it comes back to room temperature.

Light your barbecue about 40 minutes before you want to cook. Put the grill on in advance so it is hot, and make sure it is clean. When it is super hot and the coals are burning white, put the steak in the middle of the grill. Don't move or touch it, just leave it for 4 minutes. The total cooking time will depend on how thick the steak is, but I find it is usually 4–5 minutes on each side for rare to medium rare. Have a warm plate or board, and a sharp knife ready.

After 4 minutes turn the steak and just leave it in position, don't move it around. It should have taken on some lovely colour. After another 4 minutes give it a prod with your finger; if it still seems very soft and bouncy in the middle it is still too rare. Just leave it for another couple of minutes. For rare it should feel like prodding the palm of your hand at the base of your thumb, while holding your forefinger and thumb tips together. Or it should read 45-50°C on a meat thermometer. Keep prodding it and observing how it changes.

When you think the steak is ready, remove it from the grill and leave to rest somewhere warm, or on a warm board or plate with some foil loosely covering it, for 5 minutes. Resting is very important, both in life and when barbecuing meat… the meat will relax and the juices will be retained. Don't worry about it going cold, it retains the heat for quite a while, but cutting it too soon will result in a pool of blood and possibly tough meat.

Have a look at the meat and determine which way the grain, or the fibres, of the meat are running, then carve the beef in thin slices about 1cm wide, slicing across the grain of the meat, rather than parallel with it. This results in tender little strips.

Lay the tasty strips of beef in a tangled pile on a warm board, sprinkle with a little salt and serve.

My smoker is called Mr Smokerson. I went through a phase of smoking everything, such as ribs, chickens, duck, cheese, eggs, butter, nuts... there was always something on the go. I have calmed down a bit now, but if you are new to smoking, then these ribs are a good place to start as they are cheap, small and hard to get wrong. They are soft, smoky, sweet and delicious.

Smoked Pork Belly Ribs with Paprika and Marmalade

SERVES 2

- 1 tsp smoked paprika
- 1 tsp marmalade
- 1 tsp English mustard powder
- 1 tsp pepper
- 1 bay leaf, crushed
- 350g pork belly ribs, bone in

EQUIPMENT
- smoker
- apple wood chips
- meat thermometer or meat probe

Mix the paprika, marmalade, mustard powder and pepper together in a bowl, then add the crushed bay leaf. Rub this mix all over the ribs.

Light your smoker and bring the temperature up to about 115°C or 240°F (a lot of smoker instructions are in Fahrenheit) and smoke for 4 hours, keeping the temperature between 98–115°C or 210–240°F. Follow the instructions of whatever smoker you own: start with the vents open and close them down as it reaches temperature to keep in the heat and prevent it burning out too quickly. It is best to open and close them as little as possible, as you will lose smoke and heat every time you do.

I add a large handful of apple wood chips at the same time as the meat goes in; this is when it will absorb the smoky flavour as there is no crust on the meat yet.

Look out for the 'stall', which occurs when the meat reaches around 70°C. This is when the fat starts to break down and takes a lot of energy; no rise in temperature can happen for ages and you can start to flap, but just wait, the temperature will eventually get through the stall, having broken down the fat, and keep on rising.

The ribs should reach an internal temperature of around 89°C, which is when the meat has cooked, the fat has broken down and a good smoky crust has formed. Serve with mustard, coleslaw and buns.

NOTES
You don't necessarily need a smoker to make these: to cook them in the oven, preheat to160°C/325°F/Gas 3,. put the ribs in a roasting tray, pour in half a bottle of beer and cook for 21/2 hours, covered with foil.

I picked up this dressing watching a random programme about Korean food, and have used it ever since. I use it primarily on chicken, but it works well on steak or vegetables. Use it as a marinade, as a glaze or as a dressing, as it has so much depth and different flavours going on. We serve it on these barbecued chicken skewers with a side of beetroot kimchi and a gochujang aïoli.

Korean-style Chicken Skewers

Cut the chicken into bite-size pieces and place in a dish. Soak the skewers in water while you prep, to prevent them burning during cooking.

To make the dressing, whisk the soy sauce, sugar, vinegar and sesame oil together in a bowl. Add the Szechuan powder to taste – it should just be a tingle. Add half of the dressing to the chopped chicken, toss to coat and leave to marinate until you are ready to put it onto the skewers. You can leave the skewers in the fridge overnight to develop more flavour and save time.

Light the barbecue about 40 minutes before you want to start cooking. Thread the chicken pieces onto the soaked skewers, about three or four pieces per skewer. Make sure the barbecue is hot and the coals are burning white. Put the grill on in advance so it is hot and make sure it is clean.

Place the chicken on the hot grill and leave for 2–3 minutes so it can develop a nice charred crust. Turn them over and cook for the same time on the other side. You are looking for golden sticky areas of colour but keeping the chicken moist and juicy on the inside. Not moving them around allows the colour to develop and taking them off as early as possible keeps them juicy. A meat thermometer is the best way to check and it should read 65°C at the centre, any higher and they will start to dry out. Remove the skewers from the grill and leave to rest somewhere warm for a few minutes.

To serve, mix the dressing again and spoon a little more of it over the skewers, then sprinkle with the spring onions and black sesame seeds.

SERVES 4

- 4 chicken thighs, boned and skinned
- 2 tbsp light soy sauce
- 2 tbsp caster sugar
- 2 tbsp rice wine vinegar
- 2 tbsp toasted sesame oil
- shake of ground Szechuan powder
- 4 spring onions, cut into thin slices
- toasted black sesame seeds, for sprinkling

EQUIPMENT
- bamboo skewers
- barbecue
- meat thermometer

Mackerel are a sustainable, cheap fish, oily and good for you and abundant in our surrounding seas. Ask the fishmonger to scale and gut them for you. The fish will have beautiful crispy skin, but will still be juicy inside infused with the flavour of the bay. They are great with lemony mayonnaise and fresh bread, or some salsa verde and new potatoes finished on the grill.

BBQ Whole Mackerel

Rub the outside of the mackerel with olive oil and season generously with salt, including inside the cavity. Only use a little olive oil or it will make the fire flare up too much. Stuff the bay leaves into the cavity.

Light the barbecue and make sure it is hot and the coals are burning white. Put the grill on in advance so it is hot and make sure it is clean.

Lay the mackerel on the grill and cook for 3 minutes. Do not move it, as the skin is very delicate but will stay crispy and intact if undisturbed. It won't stick if you wait for it to cook through. After 3 minutes roll the mackerel over onto its other side in one motion, moving it around as little as possible and cook for 3 more minutes.

If the fire does flare up, either move the grill up to a higher position or splash on some water with your hands.

Eat immediately when it is nice and hot!

SERVES 2

• 2 whole mackerel, gutted
• 2 tsp olive oil, for rubbing
• salt
• 4 fresh bay leaves

Alternatives

sardines; herring

This is best done over an outdoor fire, you just need the capacity to start a fire, a small cast-iron frying pan, and some seaweed. We were in the far north of Scotland staying on a deserted beach in January. It was idyllic, even when the snow rolled in. We managed to flag down a little fish van and bought these huge Shetland scallops for our lunch. They were rich and smoky and you could still taste clearly the sweet soft scallop and the sea. We rushed inside to eat them just as it started to rain.

BBQ Scallops Smoked over Seaweed

SERVES 2

- 20g butter
- 6 large scallops, removed from the shell
- salt

EQUIPMENT
- live seaweed (see method)
- kindling
- fire-starting equipment
- logs

Start by cutting some fresh live seaweed from the rocks. This recipe isn't going to be possible for everyone! You shouldn't use seaweed just lying on the beach – it must be live. You can eat most of the types of seaweed found in Britain, but some aren't particularly nice. Dulse, saw-toothed wrack, gutweed and bladderwrack are the most well known and tasty.

We built a small fire among some massive rocks, where it would still get plenty of airflow from below, but was sheltered from the winds whistling in off the sea. We got it going using driftwood twigs and dried out seaweed from the beach, topped with some birch logs.

There were two stages to this recipe: the pan, then the seaweed... So once the fire was pretty strong we put some butter into the pan and heated it over the fire until it was sizzling. Then we added the scallops and cooked them for roughly 2 minutes on each side. They took on a lovely golden colour. I transferred them to a warm plate, then added a little more butter to the pan and heated it until melted, stirring up all the scraps of flavour from the base of the pan while it was heating. I removed the pan from the fire, then quickly covered the fire all over with seaweed. It shouldn't go out but conversely the flames shouldn't go through to the seaweed as this would burn the scallops. Then we placed the scallops on top and left them for about 2 minutes on each side. The seaweed began to change colour to a deep green and just as it began to catch fire and the flames began to lick through the seaweed we removed the scallops. I seasoned them with salt and drizzled hot butter from the pan over them.

Barbecues of old were often piles of charred sausages, dry chicken and blackened burgers, cooked to within a centimetre of their lives. Rarely any sign of a vegetable, except perhaps a token salad, undressed on the table. Since I started barbecuing vegetables I haven't looked back and now there will be just as many plant-based offerings on the grill as meat. All of these are made better by a pot of Romesco sauce, and possibly throw in some aïoli for good measure too!

BBQ Vegetables (including peas and new potatoes) with Romesco Sauce

BBQ VEGETABLES
• A variety of vegetables

EQUIPMENT
• roasting trays

- New Potato Skewers: Parboil new potatoes in very salty water until they are nearly done but still with a bit of bite, drain and leave them to steam-dry, then rub with oil and salt and thread onto soaked wooden skewers. Grill on the barbecue until golden and crispy, then serve, cut open, with cold butter and salt.

- Pea Pods: Rub a large bowl of fresh pea pods with oil and salt, then place them on the grill. They will steam cook inside their pods and char on the outside, they just need a couple of minutes on each side. They are a bit precarious – you may lose a few to the flames.

- Long Stem Broccoli: Rub with salt and olive oil and grill until the stems are soft and the leaves are crispy.

- Courgettes: Cut in half lengthways, then halve in length so they are big chunky pieces, then rub with oil and salt and grill until dark golden. Serve with mint and garlic chopped over them.

- Spring Onions: Rub with oil and salt and grill until charred and collapsing, they taste of sesame and nuts – delicious.

- Fennel: Cut the bulb lengthways into quarters and rub with lemon, olive oil and salt. Grill, cut-side down, until golden.

- Little Gem Lettuce: Cut in half and rub with olive oil and salt. Grill, cut-side down, until golden and starting to collapse.

- Lemons and Limes: Grill lemons and limes, cut in half, cut-side down, until they are golden brown, then squeeze over fish, salads or steaks.

Preheat the oven to 200°C/400°F/Gas 6.

Cut the peppers in half and remove the seeds and stalk, then place them, cut-side down, on a roasting tray and roast for 30 minutes, or until soft and the skin has started to blacken. On a separate tray, roast the nuts, torn bread pieces and the garlic. After 10 minutes remove the bread and nuts and give the garlic another 10–15 minutes until golden.

Leave the peppers to cool slightly, then as soon as you can handle them, remove the skins. Blitz everything together in a food processor along with the vinegar, paprika, salt and cayenne pepper, adding the olive oil, a little at a time, until you have a thick paste.

Serve with barbecued vegetables.

ROMESCO SAUCE
- 3 red peppers
- 1 large slice of sourdough bread, crusts removed and torn into smaller pieces
- 1 handful of blanched hazelnuts
- 4 garlic cloves, peeled
- 2 tbsp sherry vinegar
- 1 tbsp smoked paprika
- 1 tsp salt
- pinch of cayenne pepper
- 100 ml olive oil

EQUIPMENT
- roasting trays
- food processor

I have roasted grapes to go into salads, and discovered that they take on a sticky rich flavour and become even juicier. When we were putting together a summer six-course barbecue menu at Cook House, it occurred to me that grapes might also work on the grill. These are delicious with a hard goat's cheese or Spanish manchego.

BBQ Grapes to Go with Cheese

At the end of your barbecue when the grill is still very hot but also subdued, place small bunches of grapes onto it and leave for 5–10 minutes. They are difficult to turn depending on the size of the spacing in your grill and can get caught and fall to their deaths quite easily, so it's best to just to leave them for a while and sacrifice a few when you remove them. This way you also get a mix of burnt, charred, lightly scorched and warm grapes.

SERVES 4

- 1 bunch of red grapes, cut into smaller bunches

How To...

Pluck a Pheasant

Adrian taught me to pluck pheasants, ducks and pigeons. He had learnt from his granny when he was little. I clearly remember the first time I plucked one and gutted it – it can be quite gruesome. I think it is a good skill to have, as wild game birds are abundant in autumn and winter and are a sustainable source of meat; they are also delicious, so if you can master basic butchery you will be ready and able.

01 **If your game is fresh, you can hang it somewhere cool** for a few days to intensify the flavour. If the weather is warm or the birds have lots of obvious shot and blood, pluck them straight away.

02 **Lay down newspaper** and have a bin bag open to put the feathers straight into. Start with the breast, plucking in pinching motions moving over the skin, pulling the feathers out in the direction they grow. Pull the skin

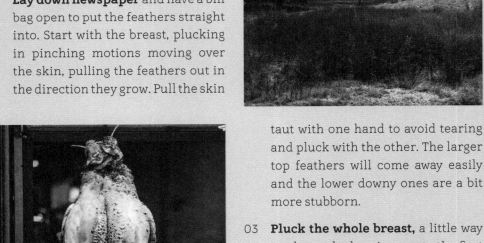

taut with one hand to avoid tearing and pluck with the other. The larger top feathers will come away easily and the lower downy ones are a bit more stubborn.

03 **Pluck the whole breast,** a little way up the neck, the wings up to the first joint, down the legs and all around the back. It takes me about twenty minutes to do a whole bird. Pull the feathers out of any shot wounds as best you can.

04 **Cut off the head, the wings near the body and the legs at the base** where the feathers finish using a very sharp knife or gaming shears and wooden board. At the neck end you may encounter seeds and leaves stored in the 'crop'. Scrape it out and discard all the feathers and mess.

05 **Face the bird towards you,** breast-side up, and make an incision, widening the vent hole. Be careful to only cut the outer skin as you don't

want to puncture the guts; it doesn't smell great!

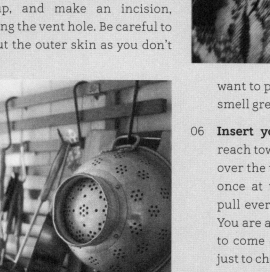

06 **Insert your first two fingers** and reach towards the back of the cavity, over the top of all the innards. Then once at the back scoop down and pull everything gently towards you. You are aiming for the whole 'pluck' to come out at once. Scoop back in just to check you've got everything.

07 **Rinse the whole bird clean** under the tap, then dry off with kitchen roll. You are now an amateur butcher.

Will Anyone Come?

Suddenly Cook House was actually ready. I had an opening day in the diary and I wasn't going to be alone anymore – I was going to have customers. I hoped!

I opened just for people I knew on the first day. My parents came, and some friends and neighbours. I prepped everything as planned in the morning and by lunch had big beautiful bowls of colourful salads ready and buttery tarts coming out of the oven.It was quite surreal, but just an extension of what I did at home, so I was pretty comfortable as a trickle of people started to arrive.

There is a little open kitchen as you enter, where I prepare everything for that day's menu. Customers can choose from the chalkboard hanging on the wall and place their order. They can see me cooking, and chat about which dish is which and ask what I'm doing. There's a stack of cookery books for people to look through and the little wood burner crackles away. One end of the containers forms a long dining space with small daytime tables. This transforms to a long table for supper clubs, with a hidden store behind. The other end houses our larder full of colourful jars of pickles, vinegars and jams. There are tables wherever they will fit and we put as many as we can outside as soon as it is warm. There are strings of little lights in the two gardens, where we grow herbs and keep the barbecue. They are both peaceful little suntraps in summer.

I started by only opening Monday to Friday for breakfast and lunch. I was going into the world of hospitality but avoiding weekends, which was perhaps naive, but it worked for me at the beginning. Mentally I could cope with this. There was, after all, only me. I was doing everything: the opening up, ordering, admin, social media, cooking, serving, cleaning, accounts and everything in between. It was what I could manage and looking back it was hard work but a good place to start.

People would observe that I had it easy, a restaurant only open for breakfast and lunch in the week, it sounded like a doddle; but I don't think they grasped that I was only one person, every single thing that needed doing had to be done by me...

Day two and actual members of the public came! I remember chuckling to myself a bit. I didn't know these people: how did they know about this strange girl making food in a shipping container? I served a small menu: big seasonal salads that you could have as a side or a main, such as courgette

with lemon, mint and feta, a summer panzanella with tomatoes and purple basil, as well as some salt beef, ham hock and pickles, and a dark chocolate and almond cake with raspberries and home-made lemonade. It was really simple, but very tasty at the same time.

I learnt as I went along. In the beginning I changed the menu almost daily, which in time I realized was stupid, really. The salads, at least, needed to stay the same over the course of a week to make my life manageable, so ordering, prep for dressings and salad toppings didn't need to be constantly changed. I tried not to waste anything at all so the menu began to take shape around this. Things are either made fresh to order or they are cooked and kept for a few days, such as roast tomatoes and peppers, or pâtés and potted meats. If something spoils after a few hours and has to go in the bin at the end of the day, then it isn't the right thing for my menu.

Cooking every week in this way has meant I have built up a huge range of recipes and ideas, which are all mostly written down in my little black recipe book. I sometimes remember something, like a tarka dal soup I was making daily for a few weeks last year, say, and then can't find it written down anywhere, which is frustrating; but the next time I make it, it will just be a variation of a memory, which is just as interesting in its own right.

I worked on my own for a year, then finally bit the bullet and employed someone and expanded to open on Saturdays too. Caroline had worked in bakeries, organic farms and restaurants and worked with me for a year. It was strange to suddenly have someone else with me in what had become a very personal space, but at the same time I learnt quickly how to delegate. Passing on as much of your knowledge as quickly and clearly as possible is something I think is very important. It allows you time and space to move forward. If everyone in the kitchen knows how to make everything, then you are free from chopping onions and have space to plan menus, meet with people about interesting projects and generally move forward. I know I have done this at a snail's pace compared to some restaurateurs, but I still think it's been the right pace for me.

After Caroline left to run her own bakery, Lou started work. On her first day Michel Roux Junior and a full Channel 4 production team came to film – talk about throwing her in at the deep end! We were asked to be part of a lovely series called *Hidden Restaurants*, where Michel visited twenty or so unusual kitchens around the UK. I filmed all day with Michel, cooking, eating, visiting the city farm to pick vegetables and chatting about food in Newcastle. It aired the following spring and was such a charming programme, full of sunshine, good food and people doing interesting and unusual things around the country.

The day after it aired was insanely busy, with instant queues forming. People had warned us to be prepared, but I hadn't really believed them so we were caught out somewhat. There was no time off for a while and there was a big shift in the way things ran. I kept waiting for it to die off and it just didn't- not for at least six months, but even then settling at a much busier level than previously. We called it the 'Roux effect', or the 'Rouge effect' after a customer who asked, 'What was that chef's name who came? Rooge? Micheal Rouge?!'

We have grown our customer base steadily since day one, the television appearance being a much bigger boost than anything else. We have, however, had great national and regional press, magazine features and radio appearances.

I remember our first review very clearly: I was in Cook House alone, checked my phone and saw that someone had tagged me with a link to a *Guardian* article. It was a review of the best cheap eats in the North, which doesn't sound very glamorous now, but I remember reading it and sitting down and being utterly over the moon, so incredibly happy. I was very proud that someone outside of the city had chosen to highlight us. It also led to many more reviews and still brings tourists to us today.

Following this I had written my secret list of yearly goals, and on it was to 'get in the *Good Food Guide* next year'. I didn't even know when it came out, but it turned out it was a few weeks later and a local chef sent me a link to an early press release that mentioned Cook House. I can't tell you how delighted I was, and desperate to get myself a copy. This turned out to not be that easy and saw my parents driving round every branch of Waitrose in the Northeast, until my mum finally got one, and got it for free much to her delight. There it was in print: *page 429 – Cook House*.

We were in the Lake District and we were just waiting for the lamb to finish cooking in a fire pit in the ground while I flicked through the guide reading what the scores meant and looking at the highlighted restaurants at the front, scanning down the Top 25 Best New Entries, and there we were... *Cook House, Newcastle*. This is still my best moment, I just couldn't believe my eyes. How did we make it there? I was so happy, and I also had a leg of lamb just out of the ground to eat.

FISH

Fish

I live twenty minutes from the North Sea; a short drive to the nearest beaches at the mouth of the river Tyne, but go twenty minutes further north and you can often find yourself on huge white beaches with only the gulls and waders for company. It's a luxury that I take for granted.

North Shields is our local fishing quay, which is home to a busy working industry alongside wet fish shops, fish and chip shops and an assortment of restaurants. It is a characterful area full of people going about their daily hard work, gulls screaming and the strong smell of the sea in the air. I like to go there as often as time allows, as I have a favourite shop that just sells fresh crab and langoustines. You can also pick up mixed catch boxes for a few pounds, as well as choose from counters overflowing with North Sea bounty. Whatever you're after, it's there, even if it's just a bag of fish and chips!

Buying fish can often be intimidating if you don't know much about it. I used to feel that way, but these are friendly hardworking people who want you to buy their fish, so don't be afraid to ask questions about what that strange-looking fish is, how to cook it or how many it will serve. They will have all the answers behind the counter. Educate yourself about where the fish you're buying is from. Fresh and local to where you are is best, as it will taste better if it hasn't been frozen, flown thousands of miles or come from a fish farm. Asking what has come in locally that day is a good place to start.

Historically, North Shields was one of many quays up and down our coastline pulling in salmon, herring, crab and prawns from the North Sea. Today it is England's largest prawn port. It always baffles me that the langoustine is not more popular here, with most of them being sold to the European market. I'll continue to champion them, however, because combined with aïoli they are one of the finest meals going…

Poached Langoustines with Aïoli

SERVES 4

- salt
- live langoustines, about 6 per person
- 2 garlic cloves, peeled
- pinch of salt
- 1 tbsp Dijon mustard
- 1 tbsp white wine vinegar
- 2 egg yolks
- olive oil (don't use extra virgin olive oil as it will be too bitter)

EQUIPMENT

- pestle and mortar or blender

Alternatives

lobster

Add 10g of salt per litre of water – the water is meant to be as salty as the sea– to your biggest pan that will fit all of the langoustines with plenty of room to manoeuvre. Bring the water to a furious boil, then slide all the langoustines in at once. Cover with a lid. Ideally it will come straight back to the boil, but you may have to wait a couple of minutes. Make sure it is on the biggest hob and the highest heat. Time 5 minutes from when the water is boiling again.

As soon as the timer goes, drain the langoustines into a colander, then leave them to steam dry. Don't be tempted to run cold water over them, as it makes them go soggy. Just spread them out as best you can in the sink or colander.

While they are cooling, make the aïoli. See page 45.

Crack your langoustines down the middle of their bellies and pull the shell open to remove the sweet meat. (Keep the shells for a stock.) Dip into the garlicky aïoli for an utter treat.

NOTES

The langoustines should be moving their claws and antennae; the more sprightly they are, the fresher they are. Before you cook them you should keep them in the fridge or pop them in the freezer for 30 minutes, which will put them into a sleep. If you can only get pre-cooked langoustines, then skip the cooking stage entirely and go straight to the eating part!

This is on my list of quick midweek dinners. It is easy to end up cooking pasta far too often when you have little time or motivation in the evening, but this is just as quick and easy – and so delicious. It also makes a good warming brunch.

Kedgeree appears in many different guises, but this is my favourite. The mixture of curried onions, cardamom rice and smoky fish is really lovely. If you cook all the elements at the same time: the rice, the onion and the eggs, this can be ready in about 15 minutes; just get everything ready to go first.

Smoked Mackerel and Spinach Kedgeree with Cardamom Rice

In a pan, cook the onion in the butter over a low heat for about 10 minutes, or until it is soft and golden. Add the curry powder and cook for another 3 minutes.

Meanwhile, put the rice in a small pan with the crushed cardamom pods and a good pinch of salt. Pour in the boiling water, cover with a lid and simmer for 8–10 minutes until the water has evaporated. Turn off the heat and leave to stand for 10 minutes, still covered.

Bring a small pan of water to a simmer. Lower in the eggs and simmer for 7 minutes. You're aiming for a soft yolk and a just-done white. When they are ready, run them under a cold tap so you can handle them and gently remove the shells.

Finally, add the spinach to the onion and allow it to wilt. Stir the rice with a fork to fluff up and separate, removing the cardamom pods at the same time, as they taste like a shot of perfume if you accidentally bite into one. Add the rice to the onions and spinach, then flake in the smoked mackerel fillet in bite-size pieces. Stir everything together thoroughly, then allow it all to warm through.

Add salt and pepper to taste and a good squeeze of lemon. Finally, place the soft eggs on the top, gently cut them in half and serve.

SERVES 2

- 1 onion, peeled and thinly sliced
- 25g butter
- 1 tsp medium curry powder
- 200g basmati rice
- 5 cardamom pods, lightly crushed
- salt and pepper
- 225ml boiling water
- 2 eggs
- 120g fresh spinach leaves
- 2 smoked peppered mackerel fillets
- 1/2 lemon

The Farne Islands sit just off the coast of Northumberland and we once put together an event with the National Trust where guests could come to the island by boat for dinner. It was one of those idyllic stories where we arranged with the fishing boats to pick up fresh mackerel from the harbour as we set sail and then plucked fresh lobsters from the lobster pots when we got to the island. Beautiful sunshine and dolphins both came into play and this mackerel tartare was one of the courses. It's such a delicious summery dish on a warm day.

Mackerel Tartare with Capers and Cucumber

Peel the cucumber and then cut in half lengthways so you can scoop out the seeds. Dice the flesh into little squares, put it into a bowl, then add 1 teaspoon salt and the sugar and set aside in the fridge.

Fillet and skin the mackerel if you have bought them whole. I really enjoy this process if I have the time. You need a very sharp knife and some patience, but I find it quite therapeutic. Alternatively, you can get someone else to do it for you, in which case this dish becomes incredibly simple.

Finely dice the mackerel, removing any bones you come across and put it in a large bowl. Drain any liquid off the cucumber and dry it with kitchen roll. Add the cucumber to the mackerel along with the capers, gherkins and shallot, then season to taste with salt and pepper. Add the olive oil and lemon juice and taste again. Finally, add the chopped herbs and mix thoroughly.

SERVES 4

- 1/2 cucumber
- salt and pepper
- 1 tsp caster sugar
- 2 very fresh mackerel or 4 fillets, skinned, if you want to avoid the hard work
- 1 handful of tiny capers
- 2 sweet sandwich gherkins, finely diced
- 1 small shallot, peeled and finely diced
- 2 tbsp extra virgin olive oil
- juice of 1/2 lemon
- 1 handful of flat-leaf parsley and dill, chopped

Alternatives

wild salmon

NOTES

The mackerel need to be incredibly fresh so make sure you speak to your fishmonger and tell them what you are planning to make.

Craster is about an hour's drive north of Newcastle and is famous for its kippers. Just a short walk up from the harbour brings you to the main smoke houses, where thousands of them are smoked daily. The herring are caught locally and oak smoked and distributed all over the country. Apparently the Royal family are partial to them for breakfast, as am I.

Craster Kippers with Butter and Toast

SERVES 2

- 2 Craster Kippers or similar
- good-quality bread, for toasting
- butter
- lemon wedges, to garnish

EQUIPMENT

- large baking tray

Preheat the grill, then place the kippers on a large baking tray and grill on each side for about 4 minutes. Toast and butter the bread while you are waiting and garnish with a lemon wedge. Pour the juices from the tray over the top of the kipper once it is on the plate and mop them up with the buttery toast.

A couple of weeks ago I drove south over the river to meet Ailsa and Rob Latimer at their fish shop in Whitburn. I tried my best to talk while eating a giant crab sandwich and eyeing the huge fish counter. Their range of fish is beautifully fresh. I came home with a bag of squid, some hot smoked salmon, fresh langoustines, some little red mullet and a John Dory.

Red mullet are relatively sustainable, as they grow quickly and mature young in UK waters. They are not overfished here like they are in the Mediterranean. So red and pretty, the flesh has a light, almost gamey flavour.

Pan-fried Red Mullet with Butter and Bay

SERVES 2

- 25g butter
- 2 red mullet, 1 per person, ask the fishmonger to gut them for you
- 2 garlic cloves, peeled and sliced
- 4 fresh bay leaves
- salt and pepper

Heat a large heavy-based frying pan and melt the butter, swirling it round to cover the pan. Stuff the garlic and bay leaves into the cavity of the fish and season all over with salt and pepper.

Place the fish into the hot pan and cook for 7 minutes on each side, spooning the melted butter over the top of them as they cook. Keep an eye on the temperature; it should be hot but not to the point of burning. Reduce the heat if it starts to smoke or colour too much.

Turn off the heat when they are done and leave to stand for a minute. Serve with bread or salad, or sautéed potatoes are good too. Just make sure you spoon over all the buttery spiced juices.

Herring have a long historical connection with the Northeast of England and my great grandfather used to have two beautiful fishing boats in Amble harbour. Unfortunately, too much of a good thing saw the fish run out and the industry decline but these versatile, if unfashionable, fish are still caught in the North Sea today. The rollmop, essentially a pickled herring, has been a staple in Northern Europe since medieval times, probably being more popular in the Baltic areas of Northern Europe than over here. The ones in this recipe are sharp with vinegar and flavoured with spices and dill so the fish tastes fresh, soft and delicious.

Rollmop Herring with Shallots

To start you need to take the fillets off each of the fish as carefully as you can, then remove any bones left in the fillets, running your fingers along the centre of the fillet to feel where they are and pulling them out with some small pliers or tweezers. Dry each of the fillets with kitchen roll, then place them into a plastic Tupperware-type container. Dissolve the salt into the cold water and pour this brine over the herring fillets, then leave for 2–3 hours.

To make the pickling mixture, place the vinegar, coriander seeds, peppercorns, bay leaves, sugar, mustard seeds and shallot in a large pan. Bring to the boil, then reduce the heat and simmer for a few minutes. Leave to cool.

When the fillets are ready to come out of the brine, dry them carefully with kitchen roll. You will need a large, sterilized Kilner jar (see page 280) or something similar that seals tightly. Roll up each of the fillets, skin-side out, from tail to head and pack them into your container tightly so they stay rolled. You can secure them with cocktail sticks to make this job easier. Place the dill in and between the fish as you pack them into the jar.

Pour over the pickling marinade, adding all of the spices, and seal the jar. Store them in the fridge for at least 3 days before eating. They will keep for a month or more, and are best between 5–10 days. The longer you leave them, the softer the fish becomes and the more pickled they will taste. Serve with brown bread and soured cream or as part of a picky lunch.

SERVES 8

- 4 herrings, ask your fishmonger to fillet them or you can try it yourself, you will still need to check for bones when you get them home
- 60g salt
- 500ml cold water
- 500ml white wine vinegar
- 12 coriander seeds
- 12 black peppercorns
- 6 bay leaves
- 2 tbsp caster sugar
- 1 tsp mustard seeds
- 1 shallot, peeled and thinly sliced
- 3 sprigs of dill

EQUIPMENT
- small pliers or tweezers
- large plastic Tupperware container
- cocktail sticks
- 1 large Kilner jar

Alternatives
mackerel

I buy my salmon from the local fishmongers, where they source it from an organic salmon farm in the sea lochs of Northwest Scotland. For the most sustainable and high-quality fish, look for sources and information that you trust and don't be afraid to ask questions!

I love this with a winter salad and some brown bread and butter, and could happily eat a whole plate as canapés topped with fresh dill. I also particularly enjoy being the one carving as you get all the scraps. The sweet, salty flavour is perfect with the earthy beetroot and dill.

Gravlax with Beetroot, Black Pepper and Dill

SERVES 15+

- 1 whole side of organic salmon, about 1.7kg
- 300g caster sugar
- 300g salt
- 15g black peppercorns, crushed with a pestle and mortar
- 1 bunch of dill, roughly chopped
- 2 fresh beetroot, peeled and grated

EQUIPMENT

- tweezers
- large plastic Tupperware container

Alternatives

sea trout; toasted fennel seeds; coriander seeds

Check the salmon gently with your fingers and remove any bones with a pair of tweezers, then cut the piece of fish into equal-length halves.

In a large bowl, combine the sugar, salt, crushed peppercorns, dill and beetroot and mix well.

You will need a Tupperware-type container that the salmon fits quite snugly in. Add about one-quarter of the mix to the base, then one piece of salmon, skin-side down, then add about two-thirds of the remaining mix and spread it over the salmon. Add the next piece of salmon, skin-side up, like a sandwich, then top with the remaining mix. You need to weigh it down. I usually slot in another Tupperware container and fill it with tins or use a plate with something heavy on top to weigh it down. Then pop in the fridge.

If you are using large pieces of fish I would cure it for about 5 days, turning both the fillets over daily and redistributing the curing mix over the fish. Smaller pieces will be ready in 3 days. When it is ready, remove the fish from the container and brush off the mix, much of which will have turned to liquid. Rinse under cold water, then dry thoroughly with kitchen roll. You will notice how much the fish has firmed up as it has cured, shedding its water and absorbing flavour. As you do this more you will learn whether you prefer the firm, very cured bits at the edge or the softer, lightly cured, almost sashimi bits in the middle and you can cure your next piece to suit.

Leave the salmon attached to its skin and carve very thin slices with a very sharp knife on a slight angle to serve.

NOTES

This works best with a large piece of fish, so is perfect to serve at Christmas or large parties. Once cured, it keeps well in the fridge so you'll have plenty of time to enjoy the leftovers.

How To...
Cold Smoke

You don't need a dedicated smoker to cold smoke ingredients, the process just needs to happen inside a contained space. If you have a smoker, great, if not you can use a barbecue with a lid. I have seen people using old filing cabinets or even a dustbin upside down with some holes drilled in the top, so use your imagination.

01 **Cold smoking is a different process** to hot smoking. You are filling a void with smoke, which in turn flavours your food, so there is no cooking involved.

02 **A little metal contraption, known as a smoking tray,** which looks like a tiny metal maze, is filled with wood sawdust and then lit at one end using a tealight. You can buy different wood sawdusts online, including oak, ash and cherry.

03 **You can remove the candle** and place the maze in the bottom of the smoker, or your chosen vessel, when the sawdust has begun to smoulder. The maze will burn for up to ten hours.

04 **Then place your chosen food** to cold smoke on a rack or on the grill, cover everything and leave to smoke.

05 **Be aware of the time of year you are doing this.** In summer butter and cheese will just melt, so you will need

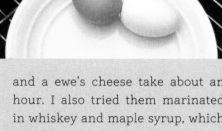
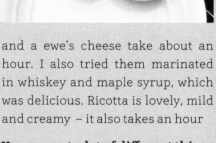

to freeze them first and smoke them as they come up to temperature. In the winter, you will have no problem. I think cold smoking is more suited to the winter months. Smoked butter is great. I have both smoked the cream to make butter and also smoked butter directly. Cream will take about thirty minutes; any longer and it will be too strong. The butter is good, very smoky, left for an hour.

06 **I have smoked cheeses;** Cheddar and a ewe's cheese take about an hour. I also tried them marinated in whiskey and maple syrup, which was delicious. Ricotta is lovely, mild and creamy – it also takes an hour

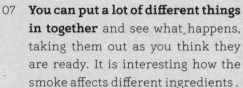

07 **You can put a lot of different things in together** and see what happens, taking them out as you think they are ready. It is interesting how the smoke affects different ingredients.

08 **You can also try eggs, nuts and fresh fish** – salmon and trout in particular. It is a fun and easy thing to experiment with.

Life in a Shipping Container

'Hi there, the menu is just up here and you can sit wherever you want,' I wonder how many times I've said that, it must be thousands. 'Various teas, a pour-over coffee and a homemade still lemonade.'

'Just in there and the light is on your right.' The same lines over and over, making people comfortable, to settle them in, to welcome them. People can look a little confused when they first arrive, because we are in a shipping container, but more often because the big front door that you have to push to get in has a pull handle on it – something that never occurred to me would be a problem, but now results in, 'It's push, just push, PUSH... sorry it's a bit stiff,' constantly.

It is quieter in the morning and busy at lunch, which is just the way I like it. It's a lovely spot for breakfast though, with the sun on the front deck. It's peaceful in the morning as you sit listening to the birds singing and wile away some quality time, then leave refreshed. We have house granola, but we also make all sorts of fruit compotes and jams depending on the season, toast, porridge with maple syrup and breakfast bowls, which I have just introduced recently on my quest to bring kefir (a fermented milk full of good gut bacteria) to the mainstream, served with fresh fruit, toasted nuts, seeds and honey – it's delicious.

People are always popping in to ask me about the place, how I set it up, if they can have a recipe for this, can they chat about a food event they would like to put on, do I want to collaborate, they have too many courgettes, do I want some? All sorts, and sometimes when I'm busy or in a bad mood I wish people would stop coming to see me, but in truth it is one of the best things about the place.

Suppliers arrive through the morning; fresh bread comes from a lady just along the road. She is from Kazakhstan but married a guy from Newcastle and has recently started her own bakery. It's really delicious. The butcher delivers free-range, local eggs and meat while the delivery man likes to chat about his life, his other jobs teaching guitar and working at festivals and the weather. The wholesale veg guy is canny but quite gruff. I miss the old guy, Richie, who was lovely and chatty. I wanted to hug him when he said he was leaving but think it might have been a step too far. I think he went to Scotland. I get organic veg from Ann and Bob in Hexham and Ann will always stop for a chat on a Thursday, about the farm, the piglets and to check how I'm getting on.

The Ouseburn is an old industrial area of Newcastle, ten minutes' walk from the city centre, a little valley with the river Ouse running through it that joins the River Tyne. It used to house cattle sheds, coal docks and lots of industrial warehouses, but is now home to creative offices, live music pubs, a city farm and artists' studios.

It's an 'up-and-coming area' and I was one of the first to start a food business there, apart from 'Carol's secret sandwich shop'. It's a lovely area – I wouldn't be anywhere else in the city. It's leafy and quiet with sounds of the river, trees, ducks, little boats, pigeon crees and the odd creative wandering around. Footfall is steadily rising but can still be low in the day. My customers are mainly people coming to me specifically rather than passing trade, so sometimes that's a bit challenging. I use the occasional quiet day to cook as much as possible, see what we have in stock and get pickling, preserving and baking, so as soon as it's busy again we're well stocked with interesting offers.

We have a city farm just down the street from us and have worked with them on various events over the years. As much as possible I like to pop over and pick from their garden – it is so fresh, but does mean I get the task of picking out all the slugs and bugs...

In the beginning my dad came every day, which was very kind and I know it's because he likes my food and is the most supportive person ever, but there's a limit to how often you want to see your parents (please forgive me), so I had to have a word. Then he took offence and didn't come back for weeks. I think we have found a balance now; actually maybe he hasn't been for a while, I think he should probably come more often!

Mark who owns the timber yard over the river comes nearly every day – he has cut down from having five lunches to himself each day to two or three. 'I'll have... the chicken, the eggs, the beef, that feta thing, a mint tea, oh and some of that cake...' nearly every day.

We get lots of local business owners, people who have studios in the valley, lawyers and bankers who walk along from the quayside, students showing their parents how cool Newcastle is, old folk out on a walk, family meet-ups, all sorts really; but genuinely all lovely people. Being in our little hidden-away spot I think it makes us quite self-selecting; people have looked us up and chosen to find us and I'd say that 99 per cent of these people are lovely, happy, foodie folk.

ROOTS &
GREENS

Roots & Greens

I highly recommend growing your own vegetables, or making friends with someone who does. The amazement I get from putting a tiny seed in the ground and then, not that long after, pulling up an actual beetroot or a full -size fennel bulb just blows my mind sometimes. And I am not, by any stretch of the imagination, a good gardener. I just plant things and hope for the best; sometimes they work, and sometimes they don't. I don't have much time to look after them so they need to fend for themselves. I also constantly get letters telling me my allotment is too untidy, like I don't already know…

The second reason, after the joy of creating plant life, is the taste! If you have only ever eaten supermarket vegetables then the taste of home-grown produce will also blow your mind. A raw broad bean out of the pod from the shops tastes of nothing, possibly chalk, straight off the plant it amazed me, sweet, bitter, fresh; I snack on them before they even get home. The fennel is so sweet and intense and you get all the long fronds to use in salads. The potatoes are absolutely delicious, earthy and rich. Radishes are an entirely different species, so very hot, fiery and peppery, as is the rocket! Baby courgettes taste of summer and peas of sweets. It is a tasty pastime when I get a chance to visit.

Give it a go if you can, even just a few pots by the back door, and if you can't it's worth looking out fresh local vegetables that will have the best chance of retaining those delicious flavours.

This is all the joy of a dauphinoise but with a bit more going on. As opposed to just rich cream spoon food, which there is nothing wrong with at all...you can serve it as a main with salad or as a side to various other dishes.

Celeriac, Caper, Crème Fraîche and Walnut Gratin

SERVES 4

- 1 whole celeriac
- 1 tbsp olive oil
- salt and pepper
- 200ml crème fraîche
- 1 handful of chopped walnuts
- 1 handful of baby capers
- 50g Gruyère, Doddington or Parmesan cheese

EQUIPMENT
- mandolin (optional)
- large baking tray
- 20-cm gratin or baking dish

Preheat the oven to 190°C/375°F/Gas 5.

Peel and chop the celeriac into quarters, then cut into thin slices, about the width of a £1 coin. You can do this by hand or using a mandolin makes it incredibly quick, just be careful of your fingers. Toss the slices into a large baking tray with the olive oil and a sprinkle of salt and pepper, then bake for 20 minutes to soften slightly.

Remove the celeriac from the oven and stir through the crème fraîche, walnuts and capers. Pack the celeriac mixture tightly into a smaller gratin or baking dish, as you would a dauphinoise, layering up the slices. When it is all in the dish pack it down gently, and grate the cheese finely over the top. Bake for a further 35 minutes until golden, then serve.

Simple and so delicious, I serve this with slow-roast pork belly and you don't need much more. Pile the potatoes and sweet fennel onto a large platter with a bowl of aïoli in the middle for dipping and cover everything with lots of chopped dill. The crispy salty potatoes are quite at home with the sweet soft sticky roast fennel.

Roast Fennel and New Potatoes with Aïoli and Dill

Preheat the oven to 200°C/400°F/Gas 6.

Throw the fennel and potatoes into a large baking tray, including all the fronds from the fennel and toss everything in a light coating of olive oil. Season with salt and pepper and roast for 40 minutes, turning all of them occasionally. When the vegetables are golden and ready, scatter with chopped dill and arrange around a bowl of aïoli.

SERVES 6

- 2 fennel bulbs, trimmed and cut into chunky pieces
- 1kg waxy new potatoes, such as Charlotte or similar, quartered or halved depending on size, skin still on
- 2 tbsp olive oil
- salt and pepper
- 1 handful of chopped dill
- 1 quantity of Aïoli (see page 43)

EQUIPMENT

- large baking tray

I originally found this recipe in a French cookbook and the amount of butter involved was insane. I've never thought something had too much butter ever before, but this defeated me. I have adapted it to suit with less butter, herbs and lemon, and it is still quite rich, but all the spring vegetables bring some balance! I only cook this in spring and summer when all those little green vegetables are at their very best – straight off the allotment is ideal!

Spring Stew with Peas, Asparagus, Broad Beans and Wild Garlic

Place the shallots in a large pan with 20g of the butter and a pinch of salt and cook slowly over a low heat for about 15 minutes, or until soft and golden.

Bring a small pan of water to the boil, add the broad beans for 30 seconds, then drain and remove their skins – unless they are very young and fresh from the garden, in which case you may not need to bother.

Throw all of the vegetables into the pan with the shallots, add another 20g of the butter and the water, then cover with a lid and cook gently for 20 minutes, stirring occasionally.

When the vegetables are done, add the remaining butter, a pinch of salt and pepper and stir through the wild garlic and herbs. Finally, add the lemon juice, a little at a time, to suit your own taste before serving.

SERVES 6

- 2 shallots, peeled and diced
- 60g butter
- salt and pepper
- 300g fresh broad beans, podded
- 2 courgettes, trimmed and cut into 1-cm dice
- 100g runner beans, cut into 2-cm lengths
- 200g fresh peas, podded
- 1 bunch of asparagus, woody ends snapped off and cut into 2-cm lengths
- 2 tbsp water
- 1 handful of wild garlic leaves or spinach
- 1 handful of parsley and mint, chopped
- juice of 1/2 lemon

This is lovely as a cold salad or a hot side depending on the time of year. The dressing and shallots can be made well in advance, then just tossed through the vegetables at the last minute. It works well with different sturdy green vegetables, such as long stem broccoli, cavolo nero or runner beans, but I like it best with French beans.

French Beans with Roast Shallots, Capers and Vinaigrette

SERVES 4 side or 2 salad

- 4 banana shallots, peeled and sliced lengthways into quarters
- olive oil, for roasting
- salt
- 300g green beans, trimmed
- 1 handful of baby capers

VINAIGRETTE
- 1 tsp Dijon mustard
- 1 tbsp cider vinegar
- salt and pepper
- extra virgin olive oil

EQUIPMENT
- baking tray

Preheat the oven to 180°C/350°F/Gas 4. Place the shallots in a baking tray and toss with a splash of olive oil and salt, then roast for 25 minutes, or until soft and collapsed with some crispy bits, stirring halfway through.

To make the vinaigrette, whisk the mustard, vinegar, salt and pepper together in a bowl, then slowly add the extra virgin olive oil, whisking all the time until it emulsifies.

Bring a large pan of water to the boil with a generous pinch of salt, add the green beans and boil vigorously until they are cooked but still have a bit of crunch, about 3 or 4 minutes. Drain, then toss them in a bowl with the vinaigrette and shallots while they are still warm so they soak up all the flavours. Add the capers and serve.

Baked mushrooms sounds like such a dreary dish, but add nutmeg, lemon and a buttery crumb and you'll think again. Even known mushroom-haters have enjoyed it. This is great surrounded by fresh salads and roasted roots with fresh tarragon, and you can also make it in small tins as individual portions.

Baked Field Mushrooms with Lemon, Nutmeg and Sourdough Crumb

Preheat the oven to 190°C/375°F/Gas 5. Snap the stems out of the mushrooms and dice them up finely, then dice up two of the whole mushrooms. Set aside.

Melt the butter in a pan over a medium heat, then add the diced mushrooms, shallots and a pinch of salt and cook gently for about 10 minutes, or until soft. Add a generous grating of fresh nutmeg, the lemon juice and salt and pepper to taste.

Lay the remaining whole mushrooms in a baking tray that they will all fit flat in, but quite tightly together, and rub oil all over them. Sprinkle with salt and pepper, then cover each mushroom with a layer of the cooked shallots and mushrooms, filling in the gaps with any remaining mix. Sprinkle the breadcrumbs over the top of the mushrooms to cover and bake for 35 minutes until soft and golden.

SERVES 4

- 10 large flat field mushrooms
- 25g butter
- 2 banana shallots, peeled and finely diced
- salt and pepper
- grating from a whole nutmeg
- juice of 1/4 lemon
- 2 slices of stale sourdough bread, blitzed into crumbs

EQUIPMENT
- baking tray

I love this bright purple addition to autumn dishes, staining your plate and bringing life and zest to brown autumnal food. It is brilliant with any number of beef or game stews, great with roast celeriac, in ham sandwiches or with Christmas lunch.

Braised Red Cabbage with Red Wine and Orange

SERVES 4 side

- 1/4 red cabbage, finely sliced on a mandolin
- 1 cooking apple, peeled, cored and diced
- 1/2 onion, peeled and diced
- 250ml cider or apple juice
- 3 tbsp balsamic vinegar
- 100g demerara sugar
- 2 large pieces of orange zest
- 1 tsp allspice
- 15g butter
- salt and pepper

EQUIPMENT
- mandolin

Place the cabbage in a large heavy-based pan with the cooking apple, onion, cider, balsamic vinegar and sugar. Add the orange zest, allspice, butter and some salt and pepper, cover with a lid and simmer very gently over a low heat for 1 hour. Taste to see if you want it sweeter or need to add more vinegar after about 10 minutes of cooking, when everybody in the pan has got to know each other.

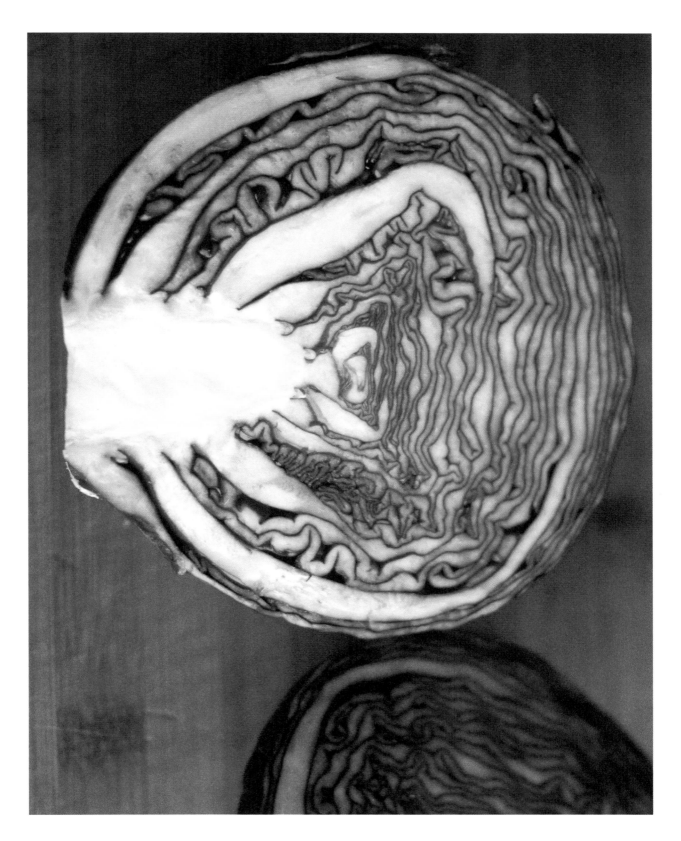

Last time we built a fire for some long and serious lamb cooking, I experimented with various vegetables thrown into the embers to see what would happen. Seasoned, buttered and wrapped in foil, I tried a whole fennel, a sweetheart cabbage, sweetcorn, potatoes and this celeriac, which very much turned out to be the star of the show. I'm a big fan of celeriac in all guises and wish people used it more.

Baked Whole Celeriac with Truffle Oil

If you are cooking this in the fire, wrap the celeriac in a couple of layers of foil and put it in the fire, right into the flames and embers. It doesn't do it any harm so don't be nervous. Leave it for 2 hours, turning occasionally.

If you are cooking this in the oven, preheat the oven to 200°C/400°F/ Gas 6, then just put the celeriac on a baking tray, no need to wrap it, and cook for 2 hours. The celeriac is done when it feels very soft to push a sharp knife or skewer through.

To serve, simply cut the celeriac in half and drizzle with truffle oil or butter and a sprinkle of salt and chopped fresh herbs. Let everyone dig in with a spoon to the soft aromatic flesh that is even better with the addition of the truffle oil.

SERVES 4 side, 2 main

• 1 large celeriac, washed
• truffle oil or butter
• salt
• fresh mixed herbs, chopped

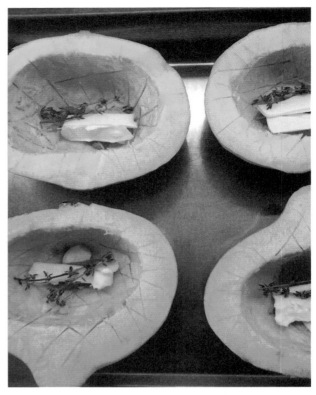

Little onion squash are perfect for this dish, one per person, or a big Crown Prince squash for a family to share – they are the blue ones with delicious orange flesh. A range of different squash seems to be readily available in the shops these days, but this also works well with boring old butternut

Squash with Sage, Barley, Pumpkin Seeds and Doddington Cheese

Preheat the oven to 180°C/350°F/Gas 4. Cut the base off each of the squash so they sit flat, then cut the tops off like a lid so you can scoop out the seeds. Discard these and scoop out any fibres too.

Rub the insides of the squash and the lids with olive oil and place them all on a baking tray. Season the insides with salt and pepper, then add half the butter to the inside of each squash, along with the crushed garlic and some torn sage leaves.

Bake the squash for 45 minutes, checking occasionally and swirling the melted butter around inside them to baste.

In a bowl, combine the barley, salt and pepper, more chopped sage, capers, pumpkin seeds, crème fraîche and grated cheese. After 45 minutes, remove the squash from the oven and add a little more butter if required, then stuff the inside with the barley mix and bake for another 10 minutes. Serve with a bitter green salad.

SERVES 2

- 2 small onion squash, about 750g each
- olive oil, for rubbing
- salt and pepper
- 25g butter
- 2 garlic cloves, peeled and roughly crushed
- 1 handful of sage leaves, torn
- 150g barley, cooked until soft in salted water
- 1 handful of baby capers
- 50g toasted pumpkin seeds
- 2 tbsp crème fraîche
- 100g Doddington or similar hard nutty cheese, grated

EQUIPMENT
- baking tray

This dish is full of taste and texture, as some of the cauliflower ends up really charred, some soft, and the same with the chickpeas. Make sure you include the cauliflower leaves, as they really crisp up and are delicious, as are the sweet cumin-spiked onions. This recipe is very easily put together and goes well as part of a picky salad lunch, or as a barbecue summer side.

Roast Cauliflower with Cumin, Red Onion and Chickpeas

SERVES 4

- 1 whole cauliflower
- 2 red onions, peeled and sliced into crescents
- olive oil, for rubbing
- 1 tbsp ground cumin
- salt and pepper
- 400g tin chickpeas, drained

EQUIPMENT
- baking tray

Preheat the oven to 200°C/400°F/Gas 6. Discard any grotty looking outer leaves from the cauliflower but keep the rest. Cut the cauliflower into bite-size pieces, including the stalk and leaves, then add it all to a large baking tray with the onions. Rub it all with olive oil, making sure you get in there with your hands and get it all over each piece.

Add the cumin, salt and pepper and the chickpeas, then stir well until all the ingredients are evenly spiced. Bake for 30–40 minutes, stirring halfway through.

Pan Haggerty is a type of Northumbrian dauphinoise. There are other regional versions that contain meat, but this is just a layered buttery potato and onion bake that you can choose to top with cheese or not. It is also delicious drizzled with truffle oil when it comes out of the oven, even though this is entirely unauthentic. It is also good with anchovies melted through the onions at the start, or you can even make it with half potatoes and half celeriac.

Pan Haggerty Potatoes with Bay

Preheat the oven to 190°C/375°F/Gas 5. Melt the butter over a low heat, in a heavy-based pan, add the onions with a big pinch of salt and cook them slowly for about 15 minutes until soft and golden.

To assemble the dish, start with a thin layer of onions in the base of the baking dish, bearing in mind they need to go between each layer of potatoes, then add a layer of potato, occasionally slotting in a bay leaf as you go and seasoning between each layer of potato. Repeat until you have used up all the ingredients. Press everything down firmly with the palms of your hands, then dot the top with little pieces of butter and season with salt and pepper.

Bake for 45–60 minutes A couple of times during cooking, remove the dish from the oven and press everything down firmly with a potato masher or fish slice or something flat, to distribute the butter back to the top. After 45 minutes pierce it with a sharp knife to check if it feels cooked all the way through, then pop it back in for another 15 minutes if not.

SERVES 4

- 30g butter
- 3 onions, peeled and thinly sliced
- salt and pepper
- 800g floury potatoes, peeled and sliced to the width of £1 coin
- 6 fresh bay leaves

EQUIPMENT
- 20-cm baking dish

Alternatives

celeriac

This is barely even a recipe, but I discovered roast broccoli last year and more people need to know about it. It brings out nutty, sesame, rich flavours that I didn't know broccoli even had. Purple sprouting broccoli is the most delicious of the broccolis I think, and is in season between February and April so get it while you can. I have since started barbecuing it, which also brings out all the same textures and flavours.

Roast Purple Sprouting Broccoli

SERVES 4

- 300g purple sprouting broccoli
- olive oil, for rubbing
- salt and pepper

EQUIPMENT
- baking tray

Preheat the oven to 200°C/400°F/Gas 6. Rub the broccoli very thoroughly with the olive oil, coating all the leaves and rubbing it into the flowery ends. This will help everything to crisp up. Put the broccoli on a baking tray, season with salt and pepper and bake for 20 minutes.

Who doesn't love a crisp? I first tried these out thinking I was being very 'cheffy', but actually they are pretty simple and really delicious. I think they are entirely worth the effort piled on top of a bit of slow-cooked oxtail (see page 131) with some mustard cream to dip them in. This recipe involves deep-frying, which used to make me a bit nervous, but if you just fry small batches in a deep pan you'll be fine. Keep a damp tea towel to hand just in case.

Paprika Parsnip Crisps

SERVES 6

- 1 litre vegetable or sunflower oil
- 2 parsnips
- salt
- smoked paprika

EQUIPMENT
- deep pan
- tongs
- slotted spoon or fish slice

Fill a deep pan one-third full of oil, then heat the oil over a high heat.

Meanwhile, peel strips off the parsnips with a vegetable peeler, the full length, and keep going all the way to the core. Test to see if the oil is hot enough by dropping in a parsnip strip. When it instantly sizzles you know it is ready.

Drop a handful of the parsnip shavings into the hot oil. It will immediately bubble up, as this is the water cooking off, give them a swirl with tongs and keep an eye on them. As they approach being ready they will bubble less and crisp up as all the water has been cooked out of them. They will turn golden quite suddenly and can burn quickly, so as soon as you see them starting to colour remove them with a large slotted spoon or fish slice and put them straight into a bowl lined with kitchen roll. This will soak up any excess oil. Make sure you have got all the scraps out, as they will burn. You can then move onto the next handful.

In between cooking the batches, sprinkle the ones that are ready with a light dusting of salt and smoked paprika. This clings better when they are still a bit warm. They should be super crisp and ready for snacking. If they are still slightly chewy you need to cook them for a touch longer. Keep them in a Tupperware container and they will stay crisp for a few days, but it's more sensible to pile them on top of some Beer-braised Oxtail and Shin Stew (see page 131) and let your guests think you are very 'cheffy'. Alternatively, eat them straight from the bowl with a beer.

How To...
Find Free Food

I started foraging for food about six or seven years ago and am always looking to learn new things. It's amazing what you see once you start looking. Buy a few books or go online. There are various apps that will tell you what you can and cannot eat. The River Cottage books are good and Roger Phillips is an expert in all things wild.

01 **The first wild garlic shoots** will emerge in February and March. . These are great to make soup, pesto or mayonnaise. You can pickle or eat the first flower buds, sprinkle the petals on salads and the little seed heads can also be pickled.

02 **Pick bags of nettles** at this time of year to add to a leek and potato soup base, then whizz it all up – so delicious! Sorrel can also be found growing in grasslands and woods.

It has a delicious lemony flavour – perfect for salads or soups.

03 **The elder bush will give you two harvests per year.** Look for their perfumed white flower heads in spring, and use them in cordials or puddings. These will be laden with deep black berries in autumn, which you can use for jams.

04 **Hawthorn blossom and rose petals make a delicious cordial.** Look out for other flowers in the garden that

will add to your summer salads, including nasturtiums, pansies, marigolds and cornflowers.

05 **Pick and dry lavender sprigs** and add them sparingly to your baking. They are great in shortbread or infused into lemon drizzle icing.

06 **I pick mushrooms from June** to late autumn. Find an expert to tag along with, as some can be deadly poisonous. Never eat anything you aren't 100 per cent sure about.

07 **Blackberries emerge in late summer.** Eat them straight from the bush or pick bagfuls to turn into jams and crumbles. Look out for wild apple trees in autumn. The more I look the more I notice them in the hedgerows. Fill a bag to make a chutney, jelly, cake or crumble. Look out for plums, pears and cherries too.

08 **Rosehips can be whizzed up and steeped** in a sugar syrup – especially good in a gin cocktail. Sloe berries can also be steeped in gin or turned into jellies.

In the Bleak Midwinter

It isn't always sunshine, fresh bread, rainbow-coloured veg and smiles, however. Each winter I say to myself, 'I'm not doing this for another winter', and each year I forget... I find myself thinking, 'Did this really happen last year?' as the leaks start, the condensation rains down, the bitter cold persists, the ice on the inside of the roof forms and the pipes freeze up.

One morning I arrived after a really cold night and the street and the decking were icy. The padlocks on the container doors were frozen solid and I didn't think I was actually going to get in for a minute. Inside I quickly got the fire going, oven on, heaters on, keeping my scarf and gloves on as I got things warming up. I was confused by a dinging sound. I knew all the strange sounds by now, from the gym, the timber yard or the birds. Ding, ding, ding... I realized it was coming from near the pickles and as I went over to look I realized what it was. The condensation on the ceiling had frozen overnight and now, as it slowly warmed up, it was defrosting and what I was hearing was the sound of rain falling inside.

It's around November time when we get the first few proper overnight frosts and the containers start to move around – the temperature making the steel boxes we call home expand and contract. This causes the join where my two containers are welded together to leak, letting in the first drips of winter. I had forgotten about it, again.

I was reminded by a stream of water suddenly pouring from the ceiling, like someone had turned a tap on, draining onto the table, seats and cushions below. By the end of the day I had five of these leaks, and a line of bowls across the room. Not great for customers' first impressions. Luckily barely anyone came in as it snowed relentlessly all day.

The fire does a great job of warming the place up once it gets going, but when it's raining from the ceiling in the larder, streaming through the roof into bowls, bouncing out of the bowls onto the floor and dripping onto the counter and occasionally my head, I have been known to shed a frustrated tear.

It is funny how things turn around though. The following week we had a really, really cold night. I arrived to new levels of cold. Icicles hung from the taps, vases were frozen, even the toilet was frozen solid and there was nothing in the kettle to even make a coffee. I quickly realised I would prefer some indoor rain!

Choosing a shipping container as a restaurant was a twist of circumstance – one that has brought much attention and good fortune. But in winter you are very much aware of the nature of your makeshift space.

Sometimes I long for normal doors, one key to get in, heating, a watertight roof; and other days I think, how boring is that?

The winter of 2018 was incredibly long and the worst one yet – so cold for such long periods of time and then the snows came. I don't remember anything like it to be honest. We ended up have to close for nearly a week in March. It reminded me how precarious it is running your own business. We can plan financially to close in January for a few weeks, but it's a different story when it's unexpected. We lost a week of trading, and then the week after when we finally thawed out, no one came. It was still bitterly cold outside and everyone was just hunkering down. I couldn't blame them; it was exactly what I wanted to do. Over the course of those three weeks we took the same money that we would normally take in one poor week and it took a long time to recover from that.

We've had other lows, our first break-in being a massive one. I had noticed something seemed odd with the branches down the side of the containers as I was opening up but didn't go to investigate. I pulled open the doors, saw some leaves on the floor and then found the rest of the mess. They had smashed

one of the tiny windows to the side and crawled in; everything was pulled out of all the drawers and shelves – a disaster. The first time they took my till and smashed it up round the back to get the cash – they could have just pressed the cash button. They also took Adrian's iPod, and a kilo bag of ground Ouseburn coffee, which I found quite confusing. I was upset as I waited for the police, but they fingerprinted everything and were quick and helpful.

On their return a month later, obviously looking for more cash, the thieves searched the place and found nothing as I had changed the systems – but again they took the coffee! The window they broke in through is tiny, really narrow, so it can only really be kids, and I'm so confused by what the kids want with huge bags of artisan ground coffee. I have to hide my coffee at night now, which is ridiculous!

The third time it happened was the following year. I just tidied up and got on with the day in an angry and determined manner; I wasn't going to let this stop me. On the plus side I didn't have to get the window cleaner out for a while: I just got a new window every four weeks or so...

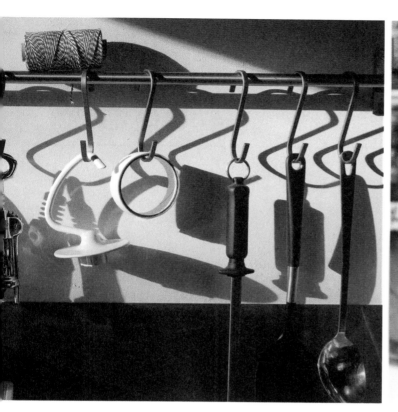

fermented Green Tomatos
29-9-17

I've learnt to fear drunken people somewhat since opening. We don't have a licence and while the bring-your-own system is fine most of the time, sometimes people do get a bit carried away. One group of women, who shall remain nameless, didn't seem to know their own limits. Over dinner they were so loud we had to shout at each other in the kitchen. On leaving, one woman tripped at the back of the room and skidded on her stomach across the length of the container. Like a game of human skittles, she took everyone else out as she slid, resulting in a pile up of ladies at the front door. I was very relieved that everyone survived and was even gladder when all their taxis arrived.

One morning I arrived to find someone had used the edge of the front decking as a toilet – in the worst possible sense. That, probably, out of everything, was one of the worst days I have had at work!

SWEET
& BAKED

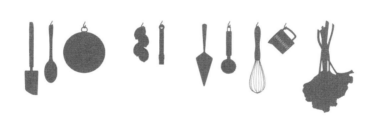

Sweet & Baked

I read a book recently which included a page of 'The Most Annoying Things People Say' and number one was: 'I'm not going to have a starter, are you?' which really had me laughing. I am actually furious if anyone utters this; it makes me doubt friendships, question family ties and wonder what on earth I am doing having dinner with this person. I'll have a starter alone if I have to. Anyway, suffice to say I am a savoury person, a starter person, a cheese person, and not a pudding person. So this is a good introduction to the sweet section of the book, isn't it?

My sweet tooth is minimal, if I hadn't already made that clear. So when it comes to puddings and cakes at Cook House I often find myself straying towards the spice cupboard, the nuts, seeds or the fresh herbs. I like those aromatic, savoury, nutty or bitter flavours to appear in my puddings, along with a pinch of salt now and again. I love bay leaves and black pepper and cardamom, bitter citrus peel, toasted seeds, tahini, vinegar or fresh ginger… I have found my enthusiasm and creativity for puddings in this way, bringing the savoury to the sweet. Pannacottas infused with bay leaves, toast or rosemary are so much more interesting than sugar and vanilla to me.

I use a lot of seasonal fruit and look forward to it arriving at different points in the year – the first rhubarb, peaches and plums are all exciting times in my kitchen. Learning to use them at the right time of year makes a huge difference – a peach in the summer, rhubarb in spring, plums in early autumn are a joy compared to other times of the year.

It took me quite a few attempts to get this right, as caramel makes me nervous. But if it goes wrong a few times there's not really any harm done and you will get the hang of it in the end, as I did. The key is to be prepared, have everything ready and in the right place. You need to pour the caramel quickly and make sure everything is oiled so you can get it as thin as possible as quickly as you can; it sets fast, so be warned!

Salted Pumpkin Seed Brittle

SERVES 10

- 100g pumpkin seeds
- oil, such as sunflower oil, for oiling
- 600g caster sugar
- splash of water
- pinch of salt
- salt flakes, for sprinkling

EQUIPMENT

- large 20 x 30-cm baking tray
- plastic spatula or palette knife

Alternatives

toasted nuts; black sesame seeds

Start by toasting the pumpkin seeds in a dry pan over a medium heat until they start to pop and crackle. Look for them starting to turn golden; the more colour they get, the nuttier they will taste. I like them a dark golden colour, but stop short of them turning black. Stir them frequently as they tend to catch quite easily.

Meanwhile, lightly oil the baking tray and a plastic spatula or palette knife and set aside.

Add the sugar to a saucepan, then stir in the water. Start to heat gently until the sugar dissolves, swirling the pan around, but avoid using a spoon as it tends to make the caramel clump up and cling to it. Increase the heat to high and watch it bubble furiously. The water will evaporate at this point but has stopped the sugar clumping up initially. Watch the sugar like a hawk. It will start to turn pale golden, then a rich golden colour; now add the pumpkin seeds and swirl them through the caramel by just moving the pan. Quickly, before it goes to the next stage, which is burnt golden, pour the mixture onto the baking tray and smooth it out as thin as you can before it sets. Sprinkle the top gently with salt flakes. Leave it to cool for half an hour before tucking in.

This is great broken up into shards and stuck into ice cream, possets or chocolate tarts. Give it a go with black sesame seeds; it's totally delicious!

NOTES

A good tip for the washing up of the caramel saucepan is to fill the pan with water and bring it back to the boil on the hob. This will melt the caramel and remove any need for angrily chipping away at the pan.

If your house is cold, like mine, I would only attempt making these in the warmer months of the year. One winter I waited days and days for the peel to air-dry and it just never happened. They are traditionally a winter treat, but they must have been invented by someone with a warm house, or an airing cupboard! They are delicious with a chocolate tart and thick cream, or served with coffee, or tied into bundles and given as a gift.

Candied Orange Peel

Top and tail the oranges and discard these discs, then score the peel vertically into 6 equal pieces with a sharp knife, cutting into the peel, stopping just before the flesh. Peel each of these segments away from the orange. You can use the orange flesh in a salad, breakfast bowl or eat just as a snack.

Cut each of the sections of peel into roughly 1-cm wide sticks, then place them in a pan of water and simmer for 15 minutes. Change the water and simmer again for another 15 minutes. Drain the peel a final time and add the 300ml water and the caster sugar to the pan and heat gently until the sugar dissolves. Return the peel to the pan and simmer gently for 45 minutes.

Drain the peel as thoroughly as you can through a sieve, catching the syrup in a bowl as it is lovely as a cordial or used in cocktails. Place the pieces of peel separately onto baking trays lined with greaseproof paper and leave them to cool completely. When they are cold toss them a few at a time in a bowl of caster sugar and lay them out again on fresh greaseproof paper, this time leaving them to air-dry for 24 hours. Store them in a sealed Tupperware when they are dry and they will keep for months.

SERVES 6

- 2 oranges
- 300ml water
- 300g caster sugar, plus extra for dusting

EQUIPMENT
- baking trays

Alternatives
lovage; lemon peel

I learnt everything I know about chocolate tarts from Simon Hopkinson, and then I added a bit of salt... I use a plain shortcrust base; sweet ones tend to have icing, sugar and eggs in the pastry, but as I lean towards something less sweet in my desserts I like to use a savoury one. The filling is enough for two shallow tarts or one very full one.

Salted Dark Chocolate Tart

SERVES 8

- 125g plain flour
- small pinch of salt
- 55g cold salted butter, cut into cubes
- 40ml very cold water

FILLING
- 200g good-quality dark chocolate (at least 70% cocoa solids)
- 150g salted butter
- 3 egg yolks
- 2 whole eggs
- 40g caster sugar

EQUIPMENT
- food processor
- 20-cm loose-bottomed tart tin
- baking beans, dried chickpeas or rice
- electric whisk

To make the pastry, sift the flour into a food processor, then add the salt and butter and blitz on high speed until you have a fine crumb. While the machine is still on, slowly pour in the water and as soon as it has all been incorporated turn the machine off. Alternatively, do this by hand, but be careful to handle the pastry as little as possible after adding the water or it will become tough. Form the pastry into a ball, wrap it in clingfilm and leave to rest in the fridge for at least an hour.

Preheat the oven to 180°C/350°F/Gas 4. Roll out the pastry as thin as you dare on a lightly floured worktop and use to line the tart tin. Trim the edges, then line the base of the pastry with a circle of greaseproof paper and fill with baking beans, dried chickpeas or rice, to stop the pastry puffing up while baking. Bake for 25 minutes. Remove the greaseproof paper and beans and set aside until you have made the filling. Put it back into the oven without the paper for a couple of minutes if it looks a bit too raw. Increase the oven temperature to 190°C/375°F/Gas 5.

To make the filling, break up the chocolate and melt in a heavy-based pan with the butter over a low heat. When it is melted, leave to cool slightly until just warm.

Beat the egg yolks, eggs and sugar together in a bowl with an electric whisk until light and fluffy. Add the chocolate mixture and beat in until combined, then pour the filling into the pastry case. Bake in the oven for 5 minutes, then leave to cool.

This is so rich, smooth and silky, just like chocolate butter. It is delicious with a dollop of crème fraîche and some Candied Orange Peel (see page 243).

There are some steps up between the pigeon lofts and some wasteland just along the road from Cook House, which at different times of the year are home to elderflowers and sloe berries, while at the top there is a field full of blackberries. This recipe came about as I needed something sweet for the menu at Cook House but had run out of eggs. A simple jam tart seemed the answer, then came the thought of crumble... If you already have pastry and jam this is one of the easiest things to make!

Blackberry Jam Crumble Tart

To make the pastry, sift the flour into a food processor, then add the salt and butter and blitz on high speed until you have a fine crumb. While the machine is still on, slowly pour in the water and as soon as it has all been incorporated turn the machine off. Alternatively, do this by hand, but be careful to handle the pastry as little as possible after adding the water or it will become tough. Form the pastry into a ball, wrap it in clingfilm and leave to rest in the fridge for at least an hour.

Preheat the oven to 200°C/400°F/Gas 6. Roll out the pastry, on a lightly floured worktop, as thin as you dare and use to line the tart tin. Trim the edges and fill with a layer of jam.

To make the crumble topping, melt the butter gently in a pan, then add in all the dry ingredients and mix with a fork until you get a crumbly mix. Sprinkle the mixture over the top of the jam and bake for 20 minutes. Serve hot or cold.

SERVES 6

- 125g plain flour
- small pinch of salt
- 55g cold salted butter, cut into cubes
- 40ml cold water
- 300g Blackberry and Lemon Jam (see page 286)

CRUMBLE TOPPING
- 60g salted butter
- 5 tbsp rolled oats
- 5 tbsp self-raising flour
- 4 tbsp caster sugar
- 3 tbsp ground almonds

EQUIPMENT
- food processor
- 20-cm loose-bottomed tart tin

The one thing that always thrives on my allotment is the apple trees. We don't have to do anything and without fail every year they are laden with fruit. Last year we pruned them right back and were rewarded with huge boughs of fruit bending over the paths and other people's allotments. I love this tart, as it's so easy and delicious. The home-made pastry is rich, buttery and warm, while soft sweet apples in the thick sugary syrup are perfumed with deep cardamom spice. I can't think of anything better for pudding on a cold autumnal day, served with a dollop of cream.

Apple and Cardamom Tart

SERVES 6

- 225g plain flour
- 120g soft salted butter
- 1 egg, beaten
- pinch of salt
- 1–2 tbsp water

FILLING
- 3 green cardamom pods
- 100g caster sugar
- 2 large cooking apples

GLAZE
- 3 tbsp caster sugar
- reserved apple peel
- 2 pieces of lemon peel

EQUIPMENT
- pestle and mortar
- 25-cm loose bottomed tart tin
- pastry brush

To make the pastry, mix the flour and butter together in a bowl with your hands, until it is like fine breadcrumbs, then add the beaten egg, salt and a splash of water (start with about a tablespoon) and bring it all together into a ball. Knead the dough gently until it comes together in a soft ball, then wrap it in clingfilm and leave to rest in the fridge while you make the filling.

Preheat the oven to 160°C/325°F/Gas 3. Finely crush the seeds from the cardamom pods in a pestle and mortar and mix with the sugar. Set aside. Peel and core the apples, keeping the peel, and slice into thin segments.

Roll out the pastry on a lightly floured work surface and use to line the tart tin. Arrange the apples in neat concentric circles on the base of the tart, then sprinkle the cardamom sugar evenly over the top. Bake for 30 minutes.

Finally, make a glaze to brush over the finished tart. Melt the sugar in a small pan with the leftover apple peel and the lemon peel until it is a sugary syrup. Use a brush to paint it over the top of the tart when it is ready and cooled.

NOTES

I make my own pastry for this recipe, but do buy ready-made if you want or if you don't have time. However, this shortcrust pastry is pretty simple and delicious if you do.

This cake started life as a lemon and Drambuie cake, a recipe that Lou who works in the kitchen at Cook House brought in. It then evolved into Campari and oranges, because Negronis... If it isn't blood orange season, which is usually December to February, regular oranges work just as well.

Blood Orange and Campari Drizzle Cake

Preheat the oven to 180°C/350°F/Gas 4 and line the cake tin with greaseproof paper. Whisk the eggs, caster sugar, cream, citrus zest, Campari, salt and butter together in a bowl, using a hand whisk. Add the poppy seeds, then sift in the flour and baking powder and whisk until smooth. Transfer the cake batter to the cake tin, level the top and bake for 50–60 minutes until a skewer or something sharp inserted into the centre comes out clean.

Meanwhile, make the drizzle. Combine the lemon juice, orange juice, Campari and icing sugar in a bowl and whisk until smooth.

When the cake is just out of the oven pierce it all over with a metal skewer; lots of holes means lots of drizzle goes in, so be patient. Slowly pour the glaze all over, trying to get as much in as possible without it running off. Cool the cake in the tin to allow the drizzle to be absorbed. You will be glad of your patience when you eat it and you get a really drizzly piece right in the middle.

SERVES 10

- 5 eggs
- 300g caster sugar
- 140ml double cream
- zest of 1 lemon
- zest of 2 oranges
- 3 tbsp Campari
- pinch of salt
- 80g salted butter, melted
- 1 tbsp poppy seeds
- 240g plain flour
- 1/2 tsp baking powder

DRIZZLE
- juice of 1 lemon
- juice of 2 oranges
- 1 tbsp Campari
- 250g icing sugar

EQUIPMENT
- 23-cm round cake tin

I have made this cake thousands of times, and it is often on the menu at Cook House as I just love it. It is rich and gooey, almost like a brownie. It also keeps for days, so is a good one to sit in the larder, if anyone still has a larder!

Dark Chocolate and Almond Cake

SERVES 10

- 200g good-quality dark chocolate (at least 70% cocoa solids)
- 250g salted butter
- 4 eggs
- 200g caster sugar
- 50g plain flour
- 50g ground almonds

EQUIPMENT
- 23-cm round cake tin
- hand whisk
- electric whisk

Preheat the oven to 170°C/340°F/Gas 4 and line the cake tin with greaseproof paper. Break up the chocolate and melt in a heavy-based pan with the butter over a very low heat. When it is melted, leave to cool slightly.

Separate the eggs into yolks and whites in different bowls, then add the caster sugar to the yolks and beat vigorously with a hand whisk until it becomes pale and fluffy. Fold in the flour and almonds. Add the chocolate mix to the bowl and whisk together until combined.

Whisk the egg whites in a clean bowl with an electric whisk until they form firm peaks. Add one large spoonful of the whites to the chocolate mix and gently fold it into the mix, then add the rest, trying to retain as much air as possible, gently folding it over and over until it is all combined.

Pour the cake batter into the cake tin and bake for 35 minutes. Give the cake tin a shake after this time. If it is still very wobbly bake it for another 5 minutes. It is meant to be soft and gooey in the middle but not still liquid. Leave the cake to cool completely in the tin before serving, as it is incredibly gooey!

I have made this cake since the very beginning of Cook House, as it works well in any season. You can use a multitude of fruits or berries and it's always good. It has notes of frangipane about it as it forms a buttery crust, but is light, moist and fruity in the middle. I just love it.

Raspberry and Almond Cake

Preheat the oven to 160°C/325°F/Gas 3 and line the tin with greaseproof paper.

Melt the butter in a pan, then leave to cool slightly. Mix the flour, baking powder and sugar together in a large bowl. Beat the eggs and the almond essence with a fork in another bowl.

Pour the butter and eggs into the dry mix, then beat everything together with a spatula. It will become quite a thick batter, but don't worry as this is how it should be.

Transfer three-quarters of the cake batter to the cake tin and spread it out to the edges, then top it with a layer of raspberries. Add the remaining cake batter in a pile in the centre – it will spread out in the oven, so don't worry. Bake for 50 minutes. It forms a lovely buttery crust but is soft and light in the centre with little pockets of fruit dotted around. Cool the cake in the tin for 30 minutes before removing.

This cake is delicious with a dollop of crème fraîche when it has cooled.

SERVES 8

- 150g salted butter, melted
- 225g self-raising flour
- 1 tsp baking powder
- 225g caster sugar
- 2 eggs
- 1/4 tsp almond extract
- 150g punnet of fresh raspberries

EQUIPMENT
- 23-cm round cake tin

Alternatives

Chopped rhubarb; apples; pears; blackberries; cherries

This pudding is Christmas in a cream, although I serve it all winter as it is so good. Think of everything that reminds you of Christmas and it's in here; citrus, booze, ginger, cinnamon, pomegranates, dried fruit, more booze…

This is great served on its own topped with some extra pomegranate seeds and toasted nuts, but is also wonderful on the side of a chocolate tart, chocolate and almond cake or Christmas pudding…

Winter Syllabub

SERVES 8

- 75g sultanas
- 4 tbsp sherry
- juice and zest of 1 orange
- juice and zest of 1 lemon
- 4 tbsp brandy
- 75g dark muscovado sugar
- 1 tsp ground cinnamon
- 1 tsp ground ginger
- 600ml double cream
- seeds of 1 pomegranate
- 2 balls of candied stem ginger, cut into small cubes

EQUIPMENT
- electric whisk

Soak the sultanas in the sherry, preferably overnight, but for as long as possible if not.

Combine the orange and lemon juices and zest in a bowl, then add the brandy, sugar, cinnamon and ginger and whisk together by hand. In a separate clean bowl, whip the cream with an electric whisk until it forms soft peaks. Be careful not to over-whip or it will curdle, then fold in the citrus and spice mix.

Deseed the pomegranate by cutting it in half and hitting the shell with a wooden spoon over a bowl, or just break it open and tease the seeds out. Add the candied ginger to the pomegranate seeds (save a few for decoration), along with the boozy sultanas and any remaining sherry, then add this to the cream and fold through until incorporated. If it is too loose just fold a bit more vigorously. Chill in the fridge to chill until ready to serve. You can make it the night before if need be. Serve in small bowls or glasses topped with more pomegranate seeds.

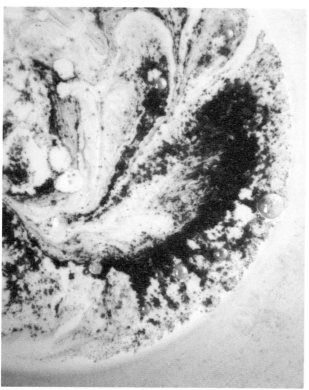

I've been making possets since I first began hosting supper clubs, as they are simple yet delicious and an easy one for large groups. You can make them well in advance and they are easy to stack into a box when you need to travel to an island or a castle for dinner!

I'm still surprised by how many people don't know what a posset is when reading the menu at Cook House. A posset is a cold, set cream pudding, traditionally flavoured with lemons and sugar. I have infused the cream with rosemary here as it gives an added delicious fragrant dimension.

Lemon and Rosemary Posset

Heat the cream gently with the sugar and rosemary until the sugar has dissolved, stirring occasionally until it comes to a gentle simmer, then simmer for 2 minutes. This allows the flavour of the rosemary to infuse into the cream. Remove and discard the rosemary. Add the lemon juice and bring the cream back to the boil, then reduce the heat and simmer for another 2 minutes. It's important to bring it to the boil each time as this aids the setting process, as does adding the lemon juice as this thickens the cream.

Pour the posset mixture into small glass tumblers or ramekins, then pop them in the fridge to set. They start to set straightaway but will need about 4 hours in the fridge or preferably overnight. They are like creamy, lemony butter when set.

Serve topped with chopped fresh strawberries or raspberries and tossed in a little lemon and sugar or a spoonful of fruit compote.

SERVES 6

- 600ml double cream
- 220g caster sugar
- 2 sprigs of rosemary
- juice of 4 lemons

EQUIPMENT
- 6 small glass tumblers or ramekins

I've re-embraced the pavlova this summer, after losing my way for a few years. This pudding can either be served pavlova style (which is great in the middle of the table for everyone to dive into), or you can make little individual meringues and serve them separately. I prefer these with raw coulis in summer, but they are also very good with cooked down autumn and winter fruits too, such as blackberries, plums or apples.

Berry Pavlova with Cherry Coulis

SERVES 8

- 4 egg whites at room temperature
- 250g caster sugar

FILLING AND TOPPING

- 200g fresh cherries, stoned
- 30g caster sugar
- juice of 1/2 lemon
- 1 handful of blanched almonds
- 600ml double cream
- 1/2 tsp almond extract
- 100g fresh cherries, stoned or other berries or topping
- mint leaves

EQUIPMENT

- 2 large baking trays
- electric whisk or stand mixer
- wire rack
- food processor
- pestle and mortar

To make the meringue, preheat the oven to 170°C/340°F/Gas 4 and line 1 large baking tray with greaseproof paper. In a very clean bowl – meringues don't like dirt or grease or anything unknown – whisk the egg whites with an electric hand whisk, or use a stand mixer. Continue to whisk until they form soft peaks, then add the sugar, a spoonful at a time, while still whisking, until it is all incorporated. It should be thick and glossy. A true test of whether it is firm enough is to hold the bowl upside down above your head – the meringue should stay in the bowl!

Draw a pencil circle around a dinner plate on the greaseproof paper on the baking tray, so it fits the tray but with some room for expansion, then spoon or pipe a large circle of meringue onto the paper. Get creative and form some peaks and patterns as you do so. Bake for 35–40 minutes. The meringue will expand and crack a little, but should come away from the paper easily when done. Remove with the paper to a wire rack to cool. Ideally, the middle will still be a bit gooey once it has cooled.

While the meringue is cooling, make the filling. Preheat the oven to 200°C/400°F/Gas 6. Place the cherries, sugar and lemon juice in a food processor and whizz into a thick purée.

Spread the almonds out on a baking tray and toast in the oven for 10 minutes until golden. Leave to cool, then bash them up in a pestle and mortar.

Whip the cream with the almond extract in a clean bowl until it forms soft peaks. Place a small dollop of the cream on a serving plate and place the meringue on top for the base; the cream will keep it in place.

Top the meringue with the cream, then the fresh cherries. Drizzle over the puréed cherries, letting it drip down the sides, and decorate with the remaining fresh cherries. Sprinkle over the crushed toasted almonds, and a few mint leaves look pretty too.

Alternatives
raspberries; strawberries; berry mix

I serve this pudding in the summer, but it works equally well all year round with different seasonal fruit. I particularly like it with the stewed plums or rhubarb.

I often put this crumble, which isn't the most elegant of puddings, on a menu when I'm struggling to think of a dessert, as I know people always love it and it's one of my favourites too.

Fromage Blanc, Strawberry Compote and Salt and Pepper Crumble

Preheat to oven to 200°C/400°F/Gas 6. Put all the ingredients for the fromage blanc, except the lemon juice, into a mixer bowl and whip on low speed to start, gradually increasing until it starts to thicken. It takes longer than you think so don't worry. Alternatively, use an electric hand whisk. Once the mixture is thick, add the lemon juice and continue to whisk for a few more minutes.

For the strawberry compote, place the strawberries in a pan, add the sugar and lemon juice and cook over a low heat for 5 minutes, stirring as the fruit cooks. Add the vinegar, then remove from the heat and leave to cool.

For the crumble, melt the butter gently in a pan. Combine all the other dry ingredients in a large baking tray, add the melted butter and stir thoroughly with a fork until combined and crumbly. Bake for 10–15 minutes, stirring halfway through.

To serve, you can either layer it up in small glasses or in three piles in little bowls or plates. It doesn't look much but is definitely one of my tastiest puddings. You can make the compote and crumble in advance as they keep for ages, but the fromage blanc is best made on the day.

SERVES 6

FROMAGE BLANC
- 150g cream cheese
- 100g double cream
- 150g full-fat natural yoghurt
- 75g caster sugar
- juice of 2 lemons

COMPOTE
- 500g fresh strawberries, hulled and chopped
- 4 tbsp caster sugar
- 2 tbsp lemon juice
- 1 tsp balsamic vinegar

CRUMBLE
- 120g butter
- 12 tbsp oats
- 8 tbsp caster sugar
- 12 tbsp self-raising flour
- 6 tbsp ground almonds
- salt and pepper

EQUIPMENT
- stand mixer or electric hand whisk
- large baking tray

Who doesn't love a crumble? Apple and blackberry was my granny's forte, and what I usually gravitate towards, but this version really delighted us one recent Sunday. It also turns out to be a very satisfying cold breakfast the following morning.

Roast Plum, Ginger and Star Anise Crumble

SERVES 8

- 500g fresh plums, stoned and chopped
- 150g caster sugar
- 200ml boiling water
- 2 star anise
- 4-cm piece of fresh ginger, peeled and grated

FOR THE CRUMBLE

- 225g plain flour
- 200g cold salted butter, cut into cubes
- 150g demerara sugar
- 75g porridge oats
- 75g ground almonds
- pinch of salt

EQUIPMENT

- 24-cm round baking dish, 4.5-cm deep

Alternatives

chopped rhubarb

Preheat the oven to 180°C/350°F/Gas 4. In a pan, combine the chopped plums, sugar, water and star anise. Bring to the boil, then reduce the heat and simmer until the plums are soft. Remove the star anise, add the grated ginger and stir to combine. Transfer the fruit mixture to the baking dish.

For the crumble, sift the flour into a large bowl and add the cubes of butter. Rub them into the flour with your hands until the mixture resembles breadcrumbs. Stir in the sugar, oats, ground almonds and salt. Give it a few squeezes with your hands to create some larger clumps, then sprinkle the crumble over the plums.

Bake for 35 minutes until golden on top. Remove from the oven and leave for 10 minutes. It is lovely served with crème fraîche or cream, and is great cold or reheated over the next few days.

I used to make these shortbreads all the time for supper clubs, as they are great on the side of a little creamy set pudding or to go with coffee and chocolates. I love shortbread in its simplest form, but the addition of walnuts is great in autumn and winter. Do try them with black pepper too. You will need to add quite a lot but you end up with an interesting warmth and spice from your sweet buttery biscuit.

Walnut Shortbread

Preheat the oven to 160°C/325°F/Gas 3 and line a baking tray with greaseproof paper. Cream the butter and sugar together in a bowl with a wooden spoon, electric whisk or stand mixer until it is pale and fluffy. Sift in the flour and mix together to form a dough, then finally add the walnuts, evenly working them into the dough. The dough is quite crumbly; this is how it is meant to be.

For small biscuits, roll out 16 balls about the size of a ping-pong ball and pop them on the lined baking tray. Slightly flatten them out with the palm of your hand , then prick them a few times with a fork. Make them double the size for large biscuits and flatten them out a little more.

Bake for 20 minutes. They should colour ever so slightly so you can tell they are cooked but they are still quite a pale biscuit. The larger biscuits will need another 5 minutes. Leave to cool before serving.

MAKES 16 small, 8 large

- 125g salted butter, softened
- 65g caster sugar
- 175g plain flour
- 65g chopped walnuts

EQUIPMENT
- baking tray
- electric whisk or stand mixer (optional)

Alternatives
black pepper

This was the first thing I made when I opened Cook House. Everywhere serves some granola with fruit and yoghurt these days, but few make it from scratch and I am yet to enjoy one more than my own. I like to vary the combination of nuts and seeds so choose whatever you prefer or have to hand. It keeps for ages in an airtight container.

Serve with milk or yoghurt and fresh fruit or fruit compote, or sprinkle it on top of creamy puddings or cheesecake, or even mix a handful through your cake or muffin batter.

Granola

FILLS 2 large jars

- 750g rolled oats
- 45g pumpkin seeds
- 4 handfuls of blanched almonds
- 4 handfuls of hazelnuts, pecans, walnuts or pistachios
- 1 handful of sunflower seeds
- 3 tbsp linseeds or chia seeds
- 6 tbsp caster sugar
- 4 pinches of salt
- 150ml honey
- 8 tbsp neutral oil, such as vegetable, sunflower or grapeseed
- 2 handfuls of raisins
- 2 handfuls of dried sour cherries, cranberries, goji berries or currants

EQUIPMENT

- large baking tray

Preheat the oven to 170°C/340°F/Gas 4. Combine all the dry ingredients, except the raisins and sour cherries, on a large baking tray, or a couple of smaller ones if you don't have one big enough and mix well.

Heat the honey and oil together in a small pan over a low heat – this is just to bring the honey and oil to a pouring consistency – then pour it over the granola mix, gently stirring it together until every grain is coated in the oil and honey. It will seem like there isn't enough to go round at first but just keep mixing.

Bake for 30–40 minutes, mixing halfway through so it gets evenly browned. I like mine quite golden as it adds lots of flavour, so keep cooking until you reach your desired toastiness.

When it is ready, remove from the oven and mix through the raisins and the sour cherries. Leave to cool, stirring the mix occasionally to stop it all sticking together. When it is completely cool, put it into sealable jars or tubs to keep it fresh.

I baked these bagels every day for months when Cook House went through a serious salt beef bagel phase. They really are a whole different species than those found in the supermarket. They are light and slightly sweet inside with a delicious chewy crust. Filled with salt beef, mustard and sweet cucumber pickle I found myself overcome with joy... one of the most satisfying meals I have ever made, if you can call a sandwich a meal, which I definitely do.

Homemade Bagels

<u>MAKES 8 bagels</u>

- 450g strong white bread flour, plus extra for dusting
- 7g fast-action dried yeast (1 packet)
- 2 tsp salt
- 250ml warm water
- 2 tbsp honey, plus an extra 3 tbsp
- 1 tbsp vegetable oil, plus extra for oiling
- 1 egg, beaten
- poppy seeds or sesame seeds, for sprinkling (optional)

EQUIPMENT
- large baking tray

Place the flour in a large bowl and add the yeast. Add the salt to the warm water with the 2 tablespoons of honey and the oil and mix together, then add to the flour and bring together into a ball of dough. It shouldn't be too sticky, but if it is, add a bit more flour. Turn out of the bowl and knead on a floured surface for 10 minutes.

Place the dough in a lightly oiled bowl, cover with clingfilm and leave to rise in a warm spot for 3 hours. When it has risen to at least double its original size, remove it from the bowl and divide the dough into 8 pieces.

Now for the bagel shaping: I found rolling them into a long thin sausage then joining the ends with a dab of water to be my preferred method. You can also make them into a ball, stick your finger through the middle and spin it around your finger a little to widen it, but I found the holes in these bagels closed up more while cooking. When you have formed your bagels put them back on a baking tray, cover with clingfilm and leave to rest at room temperature for 10 minutes. Don't leave them much longer than this; you don't want them to start to rise again. I had a disaster with one batch where the initial dough was a bit too soft and then I left them too long to rest and they were just too soft to poach or bake – I ended up with giant bagel pancakes.

While the bagels are resting, bring a large pan of water to the boil and add the remaining 3 tablespoons of honey, which gives the outside of the bagel a very slight sweetness. You can also use a dark treacle for added colour and a slightly different flavour. At the same time preheat the oven to 220°C/425°F/Gas 7.

When the bagels have finished resting you need to poach them. I did three at a time in a very large pan, but be careful not to overcrowd them. Make sure the water is simmering, then carefully pick up your bagels with both hands, one at a time, and drop them into the boiling water. They will float and bob about. You need to poach them for 1–2 minutes on the first side, then turn them and poach for a further 1–2 minutes on the other side, then using a slotted spoon transfer them to a baking tray. The longer you poach them, the chewier a crust you will achieve. They will increase in size in the water and also look like they have a slightly batter-like appearance to the outside when you take them out. Continue until they are all poached and laid out on a baking tray, then brush the top of each bagel with the beaten egg. You can also sprinkle them with poppy seeds or sesame seeds at this point if you fancy.

Bake for 20 minutes until golden brown. Cool on a wire rack when they come out of the oven.

We were buying our pork direct from a local farm last year and it was some of the most delicious pork I've ever had. It seemed only right to give this wonderful meat a freshly baked bun each morning. I wanted something between a Japanese-style milk bun and a brioche, soft and slightly sweet but one that actually held together. We served these pork buns with coriander aïoli, pickled red onions and mint. They are also great with butter and jam for breakfast – so bouncy, sweet and buttery.

Little Butter and Cardamom Buns

MAKES 10 large,
20 small

- 500g strong white bread flour, plus extra for dusting
- 7g fast-action dried yeast (1 packet)
- 75g caster sugar
- 1 tsp salt
- 1/2 tsp ground cardamom seeds
- 75g butter, softened
- 1 egg, beaten
- 250ml whole milk
- 1 egg, beaten, for eggwash
- onion seeds or sesame seeds, for sprinkling (optional)

EQUIPMENT
- stand mixer fitted with a dough hook
- baking tray

Alternatives
fennel seeds; black pepper

Get everything ready before you begin. Weigh out the flour and add the dried yeast to it in a large bowl. Weigh out the sugar and add the salt to it in a smaller bowl. Add the cardamom to the salt and sugar.

Weigh out the butter. Beat the egg in a separate bowl.

Heat the milk in a pan until warm, not hot. Test it with your finger to check. Remove from the heat and add a couple of tablespoonfuls of the warm milk into the egg, mix, then add the milk and egg back into the milk pan. Add the sugar, salt and spice and whisk until it has dissolved.

If you are using a stand mixer fitted with a dough hook, combine everything into the bowl: the flour, yeast, sugar mix, butter and milk mixture, and mix for 10 minutes.

If you are doing it by hand, combine everything in a large bowl and bring it all together with a spatula. Turn the dough out onto a floured work surface and knead for 10 minutes. It is quite a light sticky dough, so you may need to keep flouring your hands.

Bring the dough into a ball, place it in a large bowl, cover with clingfilm and leave in a warm spot for about an hour, or until it is doubled in size. It starts out about the size of a melon. The weather and temperature of the day have a huge difference on how quickly this happens. It won't take long on a warm sunny day and you'll get sick of waiting in the winter! When it has risen, knead the dough again for 10 minutes, either by hand on a floured work surface, or in the mixer.

Now it's time to form the buns. Line a baking tray with greaseproof paper.

Tip out the dough and weigh it. For tiny buns divide by 20 and for larger
buns divide by 10. If you make 10 they end up roughly the size of a burger
bun. Cut off the correct amount of dough, usually about 95g for the larger
buns, then holding your hand like a claw with the dough under it, move the
dough round in circular motions on the work surface. You might need a
little flour if it is really sticky, but I find it easier to form without. The motion
should be pushing the edges round and under and forming a neat little ball.
I then dip the bottoms in flour and place them on the lined baking tray
a few centimetres apart. Cover them with clingfilm and leave for another
30 minutes in a warm place.

Meanwhile, preheat the oven to 200°C/400°F/Gas 6. Brush the tops
with beaten egg and sprinkle on onion or sesame seeds or salt too, if you
like. Bake for about 15 minutes for the larger buns and 10 minutes for
the small. I turn the larger ones after 10 minutes if they are not browning
evenly. You want an even golden colour all over and they should sound
hollow when you tap the bottoms. Leave them to rest on a wire rack, for
30 minutes before you dive in.

How To...

Feed Five Hundred from a BBQ

People find the concept of large gatherings daunting – fourteen for Christmas dinner, twenty for a garden party, or five hundred for a barbecue. I've learnt that it isn't daunting at all as long as you have enough fridge space, big enough bowls and can do some simple maths.

01 **Practise on a smaller scale.** My menu for the five hundred was chicken skewers with gochujang aioli, charred spring onions and a sesame bun. So I made it a few times on a small scale to get to know my quantities.

02 **Weigh your dinner.** You'll see that you need 100g of chicken thigh per person, 1 tablespoon marinade per person, 15g aioli per person, 2 spring onions per person and 1 little

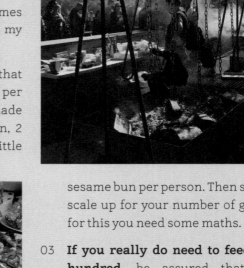

sesame bun per person. Then simply scale up for your number of guests; for this you need some maths.

03 **If you really do need to feed five hundred,** be assured that this amount of food, combined with two people, disposable plates and cutlery and a bunch of flowers will only just fit in a standard size VW golf with all the seats down.

04 **Figure out what you are going to keep everything in.** I would advise a

large range of different-sized plastic tubs that fit easily in your fridge. You may have to borrow someone else's fridge space too.

05 **You need a big barbecue,** ideally one that can be alight on one side and can have charcoal added to the other side to push along, creating a conveyor belt of fire surface, keeping it constantly hot and burning.

06 **Like any other event, be organized.** Set up a system that works and then

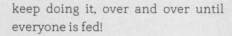

keep doing it, over and over until everyone is fed!

07 **I grilled the chicken and onions** and kept them warm in trays while Lou assembled buns and aioli, topping with chicken, onions and herbs as they were ordered. We fed five hundred people over a day and a night, barely looking up from the barbecue. It was intense!

08 **Make sure you eat too**, and get plenty of water. When it is all over drink a lot of wine!

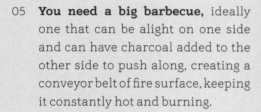
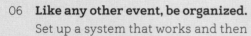

I Love My Customers

A while ago a man brought in an essay he had written about mushroom hunting. He often came for lunch with his wife or family and had noticed online that I had been out foraging for mushrooms, and wanted to pass on his knowledge. Jimmy has been collecting mushrooms in the Northeast and Scotland for years, plotting locations, documenting and photographing types he found, and recording tips on taste and cooking. He wrote an essay 'Mushrooms: Northumberland and East of Scotland' and gave a copy to his children and a copy to me, accompanied by a big bag of chanterelles. I felt quite emotional.

I'm not sure how or why it came about, but people like to bring me things at Cook House. I enjoy this, not just because I'm on the receiving end of gifts but because I've unwittingly created a place where people feel they can. I can't think of a restaurant where I would take gifts with me. It's heartwarming that the 'house' aspect of what I always envisioned has resulted in people wanting to make these small gestures.

Ever since my very first supper club, the format has always allowed people to chat about food, ideas and recipes; to ask how I made something or tell me about something they have cooked recently. It has always been the nature of the spaces I have chosen to work in and one of my favourite things about my working day.

Working in London taught me many things about how to organize myself and how to run a kitchen, but most importantly it taught me that I never wanted the kitchen to be hidden away from the customers. A situation where you are unable to say thank you to the person who has cooked for you just seems wrong to me.

The open set-up at Cook House where you are actually in my kitchen when you come for something to eat has brought about a different behaviour entirely, and one that I love.

Another man brought me an essay he had copied from the library archives about the history of my street and surrounding area. I've had gifts of redcurrants, pears, tomato plants brought back from Romania, herb plants, books, baskets of mushrooms, huge boughs of fresh bay; often things that people have grown and want to share. I've even been given a giant barbecue... although I think I'm meant to return that one at some point.

I noticed a lady sketching her family over lunch one day and a week or so later I came across the picture online as she had tagged Cook House. A few weeks later a beautiful print of her sketch arrived in the post – you can find it on the wall at Cook House. It's these little things that make you feel good about the world.

Over the past few years I have learnt that it is important not to stray too far from the idea of serving friends and family in your own home. People feel part of something, they feel welcome; and they bring gifts!

fermented Green Tomatoes
29·9·17

THE
LARDER

The Larder

There are more jars of condiments and pickles in my fridge at home than anything else. I have to get tough now and again when they are increasing to the point that there isn't room for fresh food. I love pickles and have been making them for years. My supperclubs would often start with a smörgåsbord-style starter of cured meats, cheese, salads and pickles, all home-made of course. It is a good way to serve something effortlessly that can all be prepared in advance.

My love of pickles and preserves grew from there and now we are constantly re-arranging the shelves at Cook House to make room for more. I particularly love the Sweet Cucumber Pickle (page 295), the Orange and Rosemary Marmalade (page 286) and the Pickled Beetroot (page 295). It was very hard to narrow it down to a few favourites for this book, as we currently have about thirty different pickles and jams on our shelves: shallots, cherries, salted blood oranges, pine shoots, peaches, apricots, grapes, carrots.

Homemade dairy is a lovely Sunday project. I was so excited the first time I made butter and ricotta, and it was incredibly interesting and satisfying.

This chapter includes all the things that sit in the background of meals, but will make a huge different to a roast dinner, a sandwich or a cocktail, lifting it up to new levels of deliciousness. They are lovely projects when you have some time and they will keep for months to be brought out to acclaim.

For a lot of the recipes in this chapter you will need sterilized jars. It's a stage I was sometimes lazy about, but just imagine you have spent half a day making marmalade and then the next week it is covered in mould before you get a chance to eat it! So now I am a very thorough sterilizer! It is particularly important with jams, as moulds will form much more readily on sugar-based preserves than on vinegar-based ones.

Preheat the oven to 180°C/350°F/Gas 4. Simply wash your jars thoroughly, including the plastic seal, and then put them in the oven to dry for 5 minutes. Remove the jars carefully and stand on the side to cool until you are ready to fill them. Everything is then super clean and bacteria-free and your jams, pickles and preserves will keep much longer.

Hawthorn Berry Chutney

Snip the berries from the stalks and wash them, then place them in a pan with the vinegar and salt and simmer for an hour.

Push the berry mixture through a sieve into a clean pan. You should collect about 250ml of pulp, then add the raisins, sugar, ginger and spices. Bring to the boil, then reduce the heat and simmer, uncovered, for about 15 minutes until it is fairly thick. Pour the chutney into sterilized jars (see page 280) and cover with circles of greaseproof paper before sealing with lids. Leave for a month before opening; they will keep indefinitely, but keep in the fridge once open.

MAKES 2 x 225g jars

- 1kg hawthorn berries
- 500ml cider vinegar
- 1 tsp salt
- 125g raisins
- 300g brown sugar
- 1 tsp grated fresh ginger
- 1 tsp ground nutmeg
- 1/4 tsp ground cloves
- 1/4 tsp allspice
- pepper

Smoky Plum Ketchup

Place the plums in a heavy-based pan with the remaining ingredients, except the lemon juice and bring to the boil, then reduce the heat and simmer gently for about 40 minutes, or until it is thick and jammy.

Allow the mixture to cool slightly, then transfer to a food processor and purée, adding the lemon juice at the same time. Put into sterilized bottles or jars (see page 280). This will keep in the fridge for a month or more.

MAKES 225g jar

- 600g plums, stoned and chopped
- 50ml red wine vinegar
- 30g light brown sugar
- 1 tsp salt
- 4 garlic cloves, peeled and grated
- 1 tbsp smoked paprika
- 1 tsp ground cumin
- 100ml water
- juice of 1/2 lemon

Alternatives
rhubarb

Spiced Apple Chutney

Combine the sugars, vinegar, salt and spices in a large heavy-based pan and heat through until the sugar has dissolved. Add the apples, onions, garlic and raisins and bring to the boil. Boil the mixture gently for 1–2 hours until you have a dark, jam consistency.

Remove the pan from the heat and leave the mix to stand for 20 minutes, then pour into sterilized jars (see page 280) and seal once cooled. You can eat this the next day, but it also improves with age and is best after a month or so. It is great with cheese, terrines or liver pâtés.

MAKES 2 large,
10 small jars

- 550g caster sugar
- 200g soft brown sugar
- 900ml cider vinegar
- 1 tsp salt
- 2 tbsp mustard seeds
- 1 tsp chilli flakes
- 1 tsp ground nutmeg
- 1 tsp ground pepper
- 1.2kg cooking apples, peeled, cored and cut into 1-cm dice
- 2 onions, peeled and finely diced
- 2 garlic cloves, peeled and grated
- 250g raisins

Date and Mint Jam

Combine the dates and water in a heavy-based pan and simmer for about 10 minutes, or until the dates are soft. You might have to add a splash more water but the end result should be quite thick, with the dates completely softened. Add the sugar, vinegar and cayenne pepper and cook for another 10 minutes until it is a jam-like consistency. Finally, stir in the horseradish, dried mint and Worcestershire sauce. Transfer it to sterilized jars (see page 280) if not using straight away; it will keep for a year or more.

MAKES 4 small jars

- 170g dried dates
- 125ml water or more, depending on how dry your dates are
- 100g brown sugar
- 250ml cider vinegar
- pinch of cayenne pepper
- 55g grated fresh horseradish
- 3 tbsp dried mint
- 1 tbsp Worcestershire sauce

NOTES

If you can't find fresh horseradish then this recipe still works very well without.

Blackberry and Lemon Jam

MAKES 1 large jar

- 600g fresh blackberries
- 40ml water
- 2 large pieces of lemon rind
- 2 tbsp lemon juice
- 600g caster sugar

Rinse the blackberries quickly just to remove any bugs, then put them in a heavy-based pan with the water, lemon rind and juice and simmer very gently for 15 minutes until the fruit is really soft. Add the sugar and heat over a low heat, stirring, until the sugar has dissolved, then continue to simmer for about 10 minutes until it reaches 105°C on a sugar thermometer.

Turn off the heat and leave the jam to settle for 10 minutes, before filling the sterilized jars (see page 280) and sealing once cooled. It will keep sealed until the following blackberry season.

Orange and Rosemary Marmalade

MAKES 11 small jars

- 750g Seville oranges
- 1.8 litres water
- 3 sprigs of rosemary
- 1kg caster sugar
- 500g light brown sugar
- 55ml lemon juice

Alternatives
coriander seeds

Halve and juice the oranges, keeping the juice and the pips in separate bowls. Scrape out any remaining pips when you are done, then finely slice the skin and the pith inside. How finely is up to how you like your marmalade and how lazy you are feeling. I go for a medium-style peel. Add the peel, orange juice and the water to a large heavy-based pan and leave to soak for 24 hours.

The next day, add the rosemary to the pan, then tie up the pips in a piece of muslin or j- cloth and add them to the pan too. These help aid the setting process as the pips have pectin in them. Bring to the boil, then reduce the heat and simmer for 2 hours, by which time the peel will be tender and the volume should have reduced by about one-third.

Add the sugars and lemon juice and return to the boil. Boil rapidly until the marmalade reaches 104°C on a sugar thermometer; it should take about 30 minutes. When ready, turn off the heat and leave to cool in the pan for 10 minutes before filling sterilized jars (see page 280).

NOTES
You can find Seville oranges in the shops in January and February.

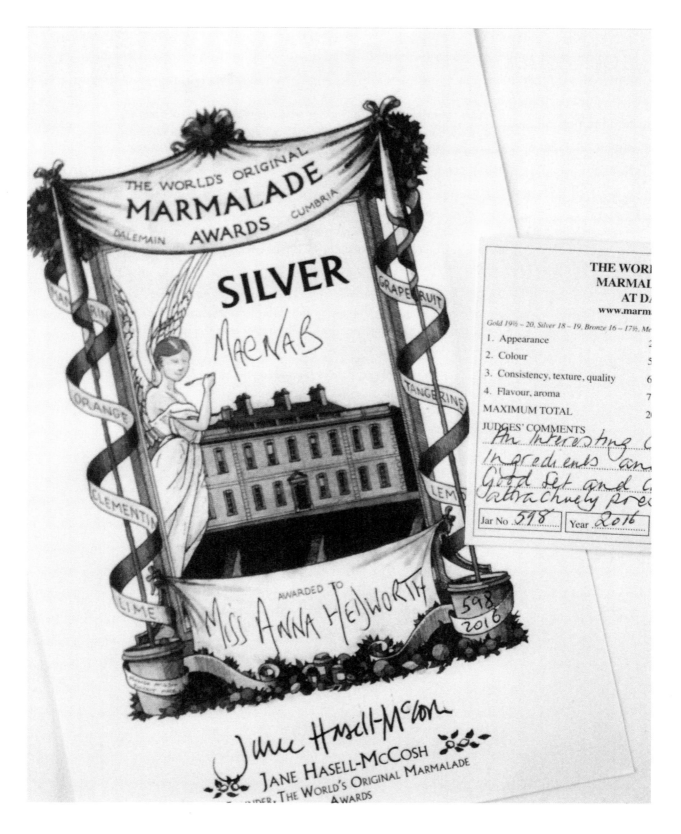

Homemade Butter

MAKES 1 large pack

• 600ml double cream
• 3/4 tsp salt

Alternatives

seaweed; whiskey; garlic;
wild garlic; anchovies; herbs

Pour the cream into a large bowl, then whip and whip until you get butter...
If you use a hand whisk it will take about 15 minutes and a bit of a sore arm,
but is by no means unachievable. If you have an electric whisk then even
better, you're in for an easy time.

First the cream thickens and will start to turn a very pale yellow. After it
reaches a very thick stage little flecks start to form in it: this is butter.
Keep beating; it will turn grainy in appearance and suddenly you will find
it sloshing around in a pool of buttermilk as it separates out.

Place the mixture in a sieve with a bowl below, to let the buttermilk drip
through, keeping the buttermilk, which you can drink or make a soda
bread from. Making your own bread and butter will make you feel very
proud; I speak from experience. Return the butter to the mixing bowl and
beat a little more, then drain again.

Take a clean bowl full of very cold water and add the butter in one big lump,
squeezing it and washing it to remove any last of the buttermilk. Change
the water a few times, washing the butter until the water stays clear. The
buttermilk makes the butter go off much quicker, so it is better to remove
it all.

Finally, add the salt. Butter keeps longer if salt is added and obviously
tastes great. Add 1/4 teaspoon for every 110g butter. From 600ml cream
I got 315g butter, so add about 3/4 teaspoon. You can add any other
flavourings at this point too, such as herbs, garlic and pepper. Wrap the
butter in little rolls of greaseproof paper, twisting each end like a sweet
wrapper.

It's so delicious, do try and make a soda bread with the buttermilk. It might
have been my imagination but that was some of the best bread and butter I
ever had the first time I made it – perhaps I was a bit giddy... it is so creamy,
smooth and lovely.

NOTES

I'll start with some things I have learnt about making butter: everything needs to be spotlessly
clean; bowls, sieves, spoons, etc. Make sure your cream is at room temperature as this will give
you a head start, so leave it out of the fridge for up to 24 hours before using. Look out for cream
that has been reduced in price – bargain homemade butter is even better.

Homemade Ricotta

Heat the milk slowly in a heavy-based saucepan. Stir gently with a wooden spoon to stop it sticking to the base of the pan. Keeping it over a medium heat, bring the milk up to 93°C, which is just below boiling point, at which point the milk will be beginning to steam and froth a little. Remove the pan from the heat immediately once it hits the right temperature, as you don't want it to boil, and add the lemon juice – you need about 40ml. Stir to distribute the lemon juice and watch as the milk instantly separates into curds and whey, it's quite exciting... If for some reason this doesn't happen make sure you have stirred it thoroughly and add a bit more lemon juice.

Add the salt at this point if you want to. I found that I prefer it without, and it also means you can use the ricotta for sweet or savoury dishes too. Leave to stand for 10 minutes, then drain the cheese through some muslin or a clean j-cloth. I tie mine to the tap and let it drip for about 10 minutes, but you can leave it for up to an hour to get a drier cheese. Now you have ricotta! Taste it while it is hot. It is much cheesier than the ricotta you buy in the shops.

Place it in a clean container and cool it in the fridge. It will keep for about a week. It is delicious and creamy, your very own cheese!

NOTES

There is little point in using skimmed or semi-skimmed milk, as it doesn't result in anything healthier or less fatty – the cheese-making process involves separating the fat out of the milk to make cheese, so you just end up with less cheese. A lady in one of my classes said she once tried it with skimmed milk and got a tablespoon of cheese from 2 litres of milk...

You can also keep the liquid whey from the process and use it for baking, just to make you feel even more virtuous than you already do with homemade cheese in the fridge.

MAKES 300g

- 1 litre organic whole milk
- juice of 1 lemon, about 40ml
- 1 tsp salt (optional)

Homemade Milk Kefir

Put the kefir grains into your chosen pot and cover with organic whole milk at a ratio of 1 part kefir grains to 3 parts milk. This will obviously just be a small amount when you start out, but they grow quickly and you will soon be trying to offload them onto anyone who shows any vague interest!

Cover the container with some muslin, a clean j-cloth or kitchen roll to stop dust or flies getting in, but allowing the kefir to breathe, and keep it at room temperature. We keep ours out on the kitchen bench along with the kombucha, which leads to some funny looks when we have guests. Approximately every 2 days, mix the kefir, then drain it through a plastic colander into a bowl. This is the liquid kefir that you can then drink. Return the grains to the cleaned pot and cover with fresh organic whole milk, and start the process again.

The kefir itself is quite tart compared to what you can buy in the shops, but if it still tastes like milk you need to leave the next batch for a little longer. Make sure you keep the kefir in the fridge once you have drained it. It keeps for a couple of weeks.

- kefir grains
- organic whole milk

NOTES

The grains grow with time so at the moment we have two large tubs full, but on starting I received roughly an amount equivalent to a teaspoon in the post. They come with instructions and everything you need to know.

We keep our kefir, which is called 'Brian' (I have no idea why) in two large plastic pots. I initially tried it in glass but he didn't seem happy.

When stirring or draining the kefir, use plastic utensils as the acids in the kefir can react with the metal.

Kefir Smoothie

Whizz up the kefir with the natural yoghurt, honey and raspberries, strawberries, cherries or blueberries (any fruit really) in a blender, and you have yourself a big glass of delicious smoothie.

SERVES 1

- 200ml kefir
- 60g full-fat natural yoghurt
- 20g honey
- 60g raspberries, strawberries, stoned cherries or blueberries

Quick Pickles

MAKES 200ml

- 100ml white wine vinegar
- 100ml caster sugar
- pinch of salt

Combine the vinegar, sugar and salt in a large bowl and stir until the sugar and salt have dissolved. Add your chosen vegetable, thinly sliced, and leave for 30–60 minutes. That's it! These are all best eaten on the same day.

- Red Onion: Great with roast belly pork and mint.

- Radish: Wonderful as a side with Korean-style Chicken Skewers (see page 161).

- Cucumber: Good in pastrami or salt beef sandwiches, or with terrines and cold meats.

- Celery: Great with cheese; add in some celery seeds too.

- Fennel: Fantastic with barbecued mackerel, fish pâtés and smoked salmon.

- Sultanas: Good with chicken liver pâté.

Sweet Cucumber Pickle

Thinly slice the cucumbers, peppers and onions using a mandolin and place in a large bowl or Tupperware container. Add the salt and mix through until the salt is evenly distributed. Cover and leave somewhere cool, such as the fridge, for 2 hours.

In a large pan that will hold all of the sliced vegetables, combine the vinegar, sugar and spices and bring to the boil.

When the vegetables have chilled thoroughly, drain the water that has come out of the vegetables, then tip the vegetables into the pickling liquid pan. Stir thoroughly until everything is combined and leave over a low heat for about 5 minutes, moving everything around. It is ready when the cucumber starts to change colour to a more olive green.

Pack into a large sterilized kilner jar (see page 280), packing it down as you fill it up so you get as much in as possible. It is ready to eat the next day. I like it young but it also keeps well.

MAKES 1 large jar

- 3 cucumbers
- 3 green peppers
- 3 onions
- 60g salt
- 240ml white wine vinegar
- 200g caster sugar
- 1/2 tsp ground turmeric
- 1/2 tsp celery seeds
- 2 tbsp mustard seeds
- 2 tbsp coriander seeds

Pickled Beetroot with Juniper, Orange and Chilli

Heat the water, vinegar, salt and sugar together in a large pan until the sugar has dissolved, then add the orange zest, peppercorns, chilli flakes and juniper berries. Bring to a low simmer.

Peel the raw beetroot (you may want to wear rubber gloves), then cut into 1-cm wide slices. Cut these slices into 1-cm wide batons and pack these as tightly as you can into large sterilized kilner jars (see page 280). Pour over the hot spiced pickling liquid and seal the jar once cooled. Leave the pickles for at least a week before eating.

MAKES 2 large jars

- 750ml water
- 500ml cider vinegar
- 15g salt
- 350g caster sugar
- 4 large strips of orange zest
- 6 peppercorns
- 1/2 tsp chilli flakes
- 3 juniper berries, crushed
- 1kg beetroot

Alternatives
rhubarb; cherries

Fermented Turnip with Bay and Beetroot

MAKES 1 large jar

- 750ml water
- 70g salt
- 2 bay leaves
- 250ml white wine vinegar
- 3 garlic cloves, peeled
- 1kg turnip or swede, peeled and cut into 1-cm batons
- 1 small beetroot, peeled and cut into 1-cm batons

Combine the water, salt and bay leaves in a large pan and bring to the boil, then add the vinegar and garlic and return to the boil.

Pack the turnip and beetroot batons into a sterilized Kilner jar (see page 280) as tightly as you can. Make sure the beetroot is distributed throughout, then pour over the hot pickling liquid. Push the vegetables down so they are submerged under the liquid and seal while hot. Store it at room temperature for a week before opening.

Pickled Green Tomatoes with Chilli and Garlic

MAKES 2-litre jar

- 600g green tomatoes
- 1 garlic clove, peeled and sliced
- 1 handful of celery leaves, chopped
- 1 red chilli, sliced
- 500ml water
- 500ml white wine vinegar
- 2 tbsp salt
- 2 tbsp caster sugar
- 1 tbsp coriander seeds
- 1 tbsp celery seeds

Cut the tomatoes into quarters or even smaller segments if they are big. Pack them into the sterilized jar (see page 280) with the sliced garlic, celery leaves and chilli slices distributed throughout.

Combine the water, vinegar, salt, sugar and spices in a pan and bring to the boil, then pour the hot pickling liquid over the tomatoes. Push them down so they are submerged under the liquid and seal the jar. They will be ready after three days and keep for six months or more.

Flavoured Vinegars

There is no measured recipe to this section other than put things in vinegar! The pine shoot vinegar is definitely my favourite over the years. I have also made apricot and ginger, lovage and parsley, elderflower, elderberry... you can add peppercorns, rosemary, bay leaves, garlic or citrus peel, if you like.

I fill about half of the jar with my chosen ingredients and then fill with white wine, cider or red wine vinegar to the brim. I usually use white wine vinegar as I feel the flavours of the ingredients come through more. Make sure your jars are sterilized (see page 280).

Leave somewhere dark for about two weeks, shaking the jar every few days. If using delicate ingredients, such as fruit or flowers, then strain the vinegar at this point and store without the fruit or flowers in it. However, ingredients such as pine or garlic or woody herbs can stay in and will only improve the flavour. They all keep for at least a year.

These flavoured vinegars are great used in salad dressings, such as tarragon vinegar on a roast chicken salad, or even to make a béarnaise sauce, or elderflower vinegar in a dressing over melon and cured ham. You can also add a splash of elderberry at the end of a game stew or some peach or fennel vinegar into slow-braised pork. Add a teaspoon to the end of a fruit compote to lift the flavours; ginger is great in a strawberry or rhubarb compote. I like the pine shoot vinegar in a cocktail, just a dash, along with many of the others, such as ginger, fennel, elderflower...

- pine shoots
- fennel
- elderflower
- lovage
- tarragon
- ginger
- elderberry

Cherry Shrub

Cherry was my first shrub experiment. Wash whatever fruit you are going to use. I stoned a load of big fat cherries, about half a large Kilner jar full. Just tear them in half into a bowl, then mash them up either with your hands or a potato masher, crushing the flesh and getting all the juices moving. Add them to the jar, then add roughly the same quantity of vinegar to fruit. I don't think you need to be super accurate. Seal the jar and shake well, then leave for 1–2 weeks, shaking the jar every few days. You want the maximum amount of fruit flavour to come out as possible.

Then it is time to strain the fruit mix and add the sugar. Strain it through some muslin or a sieve. It is fine if a bit of pulp stays in the mix, it's just down to preference. Then add sugar to taste. I add about half as much sugar to liquid – some recipes say equal amounts, but I find this is far too sweet. I want to taste the fruit, not just sugar. If you have about 1 litre fruit vinegar then add about 500ml by volume of caster sugar. You don't need any heat, just stir until it is dissolved, then it is ready to use.

To drink, I use 1 part shrub to 5 parts soda or water, or gin... but it is down to personal taste really. I'm a total vinegar-drinking convert now and I hope you feel the same.

MAKES 2-litre jar

- 500g fresh cherries, about 1/2 a jar
- 1 litre organic white wine vinegar
- about 500ml caster sugar by volume

Alternatives

cherry and rosemary; gooseberry; rhubarb and orange; elderflower; strawberry and black pepper; pine shoot; blood orange and lemon verbena; apricot and ginger

Rosehip Syrup

MAKES 1.5 litres

- 500g rosehips
- 800ml boiling water
- 500g granulated sugar

I picked about three or four large handfuls of rosehips, which came to about 500g. Wash them carefully, getting rid of dirt, chaff and bugs. Blitz in a food processor until quite fine, then transfer to a pan and add the boiling water. Bring to the boil briefly, then remove the pan from the heat and leave to stand for about 30 minutes.

Pour the mixture through a jelly bag or muslin cloth set over a colander and leave to drip for an hour. Squeeze all the liquid out gently, being careful not to split the cloth. There should be about 900ml of juice.

Combine the juice with the sugar in a large pan and heat over a low heat until dissolved. Bring to the boil and boil for 3 minutes, then pour into sterilized bottles or jars (see page 280) and store in the fridge. It will keep for about four months.

Hawthorn Blossom Syrup

MAKES 2 litres

- 1 litre picked hawthorn blossoms
- 800g caster sugar, plus extra for packing
- 1.25 litres water
- 7 tbsp lemon juice

I picked a carrier bag full of lovely white blossoms. You need about 1 litre of blossoms. Gently snip the flowers from the stalks and pack them loosely into sterilized kilner jars (see page 280) in layers about 2.5cm deep. Sprinkle 1 teaspoon of sugar between each layer of flowers, until the jars are full.

In a pan, bring the 800g sugar, water and lemon juice to the boil and boil for 3 minutes, then allow to cool.

Pour the cooled syrup into the jar with the flowers and put the lids on loosely. Stand the jars in a large pan on top of a few sheets of folded newspaper, with some newspaper between the jars so they don't touch. Fill up the pan with cold water and bring to the boil slowly. Reduce the heat and simmer very gently for 1 hour.

Carefully lift out the jars using a cloth, and tighten the lids. When everything is stone-cold open the jars and strain the flowers from the syrup through a muslin cloth into sterilized jars or bottles. Seal and keep somewhere cool. It will keep for months.

It's a delicious apricot-coloured syrup. Serve with soda, ice and a squeeze of lemon with a few flowers scattered on top. It's also good with gin and tonic or drizzled over pannacotta or ice cream.

Still Lemonade

Heat the water and sugar together gently in a large pan, stirring so the sugar doesn't all clump at the bottom. Once the sugar has dissolved, bring to the boil, then remove the pan from the heat and leave to cool slightly before adding the lemon juice. If there are any pips left in by accident they will float to the top because of the warmth, so scoop them out.

You can now bottle the lemonade into sterilized bottles (see page 280) and keep it in the fridge. It is a cordial so will need diluting before serving. I use one part lemonade to three parts chilled water or soda. It's great with gin and soda!

MAKES 4 litres

- 2 litres water
- 2 litres caster sugar by volume
- 800ml lemon juice, about 14 lemons

Elderflower Gin

Shake the bugs from the elderflowers off outside, then add the flowers to a bottle of gin with 3–4 large strips of lemon zest. Leave somewhere cool for 24–48 hours, then strain through a muslin cloth. The gin will keep indefinitely. Serve with soda and a dash of homemade Still Lemonade (see above), or tonic.

MAKES 1 bottle

- 6–7 full heads of elderflowers
- 1 bottle of gin
- zest of 1 lemon

NOTES
Elderflowers are best picked on a sunny day, which sounds a bit like folklore, but the rain will alter their flavour. I think a grey day is probably fine!

Kombucha

MAKES 2 litres

- 2 litres water
- 7 tea bags, I like green, but you can use any
- 170g caster sugar
- 1 scoby (symbiotic community of bacteria and yeast)

To start, simply brew a big batch of strong sugary tea. I used 2 litres water, 7 teabags and 170g caster sugar. I have used breakfast tea in the past, but currently favour green tea as it makes a lighter, more refreshing drink. Boil the water in a pan, add the sugar and stir until it has dissolved. Add the teabags and leave the tea to brew for 30 minutes, then remove the teabags and leave the tea to cool.

Kombucha doesn't like metal or plastic, as the acids in it can react with these materials over time, so it is best to keep it in a large glass jar. You can also see what is going on then. I use a plastic spoon to stir it, as the contact is very minimal. Transfer the tea to the jar, and add the scoby. The tea needs to be open to the air, but to avoid dust or fruit flies getting in, I cover the top of mine with some kitchen roll and an elastic band. Keep it at room temperature. Mine is just on the bench in the kitchen – it's a bit of a talking point!

It is ready when it no longer tastes of tea. The fermentation process feeds on the sugar so it is no longer sweet, almost like a tart apple juice, a slightly cider-like taste. The first batch will take the longest as the scoby will take some time to get going. It is also dependent on the weather so mine will ferment quicker in summer and slower in winter. My first batch took a month, and in the summer it can be ready in a week. I currently make 4-litre jars at a time, which take longer. I would check on it after 4 days and keep checking every few days after that. If it starts to taste very acidic, like vinegar, it has been left too long. There is no harm done and you can still drink it like this, it's just an acquired taste, but simply start the process again.

Pour off the kombucha into clean, sterilized bottles (see page 280) leaving behind the scoby and a cup of kombucha in the bottom of the jar, which will start your next batch fermenting, then begin the process again, brewing a new batch of tea and adding it in with the scoby when it is cool. It is a constant cycle. You will notice that it has developed a light fizz too.

As your scoby gets used to its surroundings it will start to grow baby scobys. These may form as a thin new skin over the top of the liquid or attached to the underside of your original scoby. Just leave them in and once they are the thickness of your original scoby, gently remove them and use them in another jar to start another batch, or give them to friends as very strange gifts!

Once you have strained off the kombucha you can flavour it. I like it as it is, but you can add fruit, such as apples, oranges, plums, pears, ginger... leave it for a further week at room temperature, where it will continue to ferment, then strain again and drink. You can use the fruit in salads or puddings too.

Keep the kombucha in the fridge once it is ready. This will stop the fermentation process; it becomes too vinegary if left for too long. I find it delicious and such a great soft drink that isn't sickly sweet as most commercial soft drinks are. It is very refreshing with ice and fresh mint, and reassuring that you are feeding lots of good bacteria to your gut too.

NOTES

A Scoby is a 'symbiotic community of bacteria and yeast', a living thing that ferments your tea, turning it into a refreshing sharp drink not dissimilar to apple juice or cider. I ordered my 'scoby' online. It looks a bit like the contents of a petri dish – a bit weird! It arrived in a pouch with a little bit of kombucha liquid, already fermented, which is full of live microbes and helps gets your batch started.

How To...
Build a Beach Fire

There's no better joy in life than a small fire on the beach to me, even more so if you have something to cook on it. I expand my outdoor cooking repertoire every summer, trying out a new project whenever possible. To be honest, though, you should not let the seasons hold you back. We took a winter break up at the top of Scotland on a tiny beach and had a little fire going on day one.

01 **Identify your camp**, somewhere a bit sheltered and above the high tide mark with surrounding flat areas for sitting.

02 **Choose your fireplace.** In among rocks will get some air flow through the fire, or dig a hole in the sand, make a bed of different-sized rocks and build a ring of surrounding rocks to protect the fire from the wind and stop it spreading.

03 **Grab some blankets:** to sit on in

summer, or wrap round you in winter!

04 **Create your sitting area** using rocks or driftwood or make some chairs in the sand.

05 **Gather your fuel:** you will need a range from dry grass, dry seaweed, tiny twigs or newspaper, to medium twigs, larger twigs and branches to large pieces of driftwood or logs. You will need some matches, a lighter or a

 blowtorch, unless you fancy yourself as a flint-wielding fire starter…

06 **Build the fire** initially from grass and small twigs, with some larger pieces of wood arranged like a tepee above – lots of air flow is key. Light the grasses and gradually add more twigs and wood as it gets going, keeping it in a tepee shape to help it to keep burning. Take some fire lighters just in case the fire doesn't catch; it can prevent arguments.

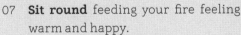

07 **Sit round** feeding your fire feeling warm and happy.

08 **Throw on some food!** Try meat threaded onto skewers or twigs, foil-wrapped fish or veg with some butter. Marshmallows, buns, sausages, new potatoes and bacon are all good ideas! Cook on a small grill or metal pan balanced on the edge of the fire or go all Bear Grylls and make a tripod out of long sticks and hang your food by the fire – (See Fire recipe chapter for advice). Relax and poke the fire.

Cook House: The Future

Cook House is about cooking good food that's interesting and delicious in a happy, relaxed environment, with good music and nice people making you feel at ease and comfortable. It is about meeting new people, talking to each other about food, recipes and where you're from. It is about shared experience and conviviality. It is about learning more about where your food comes from, who grew it and how to make it. It's about motivation to make my neighbourhood and city a better place. It is about reminding people that eating out is personal, and it's about the people cooking, eating and growing, which you shouldn't forget. It's also about a passion to do something I love for a living and to encourage others to do the same. I get very excited when I hear people say, 'I'm thinking about leaving my job to do this...'

My constant motivation is seeing people enjoy themselves with good food, smiling and laughing and clinking glasses. I am inspired to plan the dinners I want to go to, the restaurants I want to visit, the events I want to attend. Unfortunately that means that I never get to experience them as a guest! I do think I take just as much pleasure in seeing other people enjoy them, however. And one day maybe we will have grown enough as a business that I can be a guest too! I definitely don't want to be the one doing the washing up in a few years' time...

By opening Cook House in a very small first venue I have learnt how to do so much in real time. I have made it all up as I've gone along, working hard and learning as I go. I have learnt how I can improve and what I want to achieve in the future, as well as how to make bread, butter, cheese, salami, pickles, pies – and much more!

Cook House still offers exactly the same thing it did on day one: a warm welcome and some delicious food in an interesting space. It has also come so far and it has been an organic growth. 'Slow and steady wins the race' is what they say, and I think that's definitely true when finding your feet in a new business and a new profession. Take your time.

I did not know I would be writing a book on our four-year anniversary, or that I would cook on national television with Michel Roux Junior, or that we would make it into the Good Food Guide and be listed in the best new entries, or that people would love our food and queue out the door for it!

Today I am in the process of expanding Cook House and that means moving to a new venue. It is a much bigger project and I am currently experiencing all those fears I had the first time round. They are the same questions: What if I can't do this? What if I don't have enough money? How do I cook that? How will the service work? I managed then, so I know (and hope) I will manage again. I want to challenge myself and continue to learn and embrace change. As a relatively new restaurateur and cook I am always looking for new ideas and inspiration, and to find like minds. I read, I cook, I ask other chefs for advice, I try out anything that makes me curious and excited, and I keep doing that over and over; things move forward and evolve, and new opportunities and ideas keep coming along.

My purpose in writing this book has always been to inspire people to do what they always wondered if they could: open a café or a cake shop; be a baker or a florist; train to be a chef; start a street-food cart; whatever it is I would very much advise that you give it a go, change your life and do the stuff that you love as a profession. Start small – it won't happen overnight, but imagine what you would like your life to be and start working towards it!

I have made my own way so far. You don't have to pigeonhole yourself into a traditional job and, looking back, I'm glad that I was brave enough to just do my own thing. It didn't feel like I was being brave at the time, naive perhaps; I just couldn't ignore my desire to create something that people would enjoy, which I would enjoy, and which one step at a time all joined up to become a job.

Acknowledgements

I always had pipe dreams of writing a book, so first thank you must go to Daisy Parente my agent for spotting this might be a thing. Thank you to Ellen Parnavelas my editor at Head of Zeus for giving me this chance and being so supportive. Jessie for designing such a beautiful book and Heather for stepping into the breach.

Thank you to people in the food world for welcoming, encouraging and inspiring me when I was just starting out and to the present day; namely Alison Swan Parente, Olia Hercules, Jeremy Lee, Bee Wilson, Margot Henderson, Anna Tobias, Rachel Roddy, James Whetlor and Michel Roux Jnr for being both inspiring and encouraging.

Words of help, advice and encouragement were readily available locally and I am very grateful to Tony Renwick, Shaun Hurrell, Terry Laybourne, Nick Grieves, Charlotte Harbottle, for taking the time to help me when I was starting out.

Thank you to photographers Garrod Kirkwood, Wiesia Bjoko & James Byrne who have captured and shown an interest in the place from the beginning. Taking charge of the other photos for the book was entirely terrifying, I'm so glad I had your talents to supplement. To Caroline, and then Lou for allowing me time away from the restaurant to actually write a book; Lou is the best right-hand woman you could wish for and has become indispensible, a hilarious joy and talent. And everybody in the Cook House team today, you are the best. To all my lovely customers who have supported Cook House from the beginning, thank you for coming; a thank you from you and a couple of kind words are the reason I do all of this. To my parents, sister, family and best friends for being such willing recipients of all food and drinks I decide I want to try out, it's a tough job but someone has to mop it up.

To Adrian for being my harshest critic and biggest supporter, he is always striving for everything to be perfect and spurs me on even when I feel deflated. I wouldn't have been able to do any of this without him. I count myself very lucky to have found such a lovely partner in cooking and life, and to Flo for being amazing (she made me say that).

To all the cookbooks I've read and restaurants I've eaten in and enjoyed, for making me want to achieve something great.

To food that makes you laugh with joy, as really, that's what it is all about.

Index